JEN WILKIN

ABIDE

Lifeway Press®
Brentwood, Tennessee

EDITORIAL TEAM, LIFEWAY WOMEN BIBLE STUDIES

Becky Loyd
Director, Lifeway Women

Tina Boesch
Manager

Chelsea Waack
Production Leader

Laura Magness
Content Editor

Tessa Morrell
Production Editor

Lauren Ervin
Graphic Designer

Micah Kandros
Cover Design

Published by Lifeway Press® • © 2023 Jen Wilkin

Reprinted June 2023

ISBN: 978-1-0877-6880-9

Item: 005838414

Dewey Decimal Classification: 227.94
Subject Headings: BIBLE. N.T. JOHN (EPISTLES) / FAITH / CHRISTIAN LIFE

Unless otherwise indicated, all Scripture quotations are from the ESV® Bible (The Holy Bible, English Standard Version®), copyright © 2001 by Crossway, a publishing ministry of Good News Publishers. Used by permission. All rights reserved. The ESV text may not be quoted in any publication made available to the public by a Creative Commons license. The ESV may not be translated into any other language.

English Standard Version, ESV, and the ESV logo are registered trademarks of Good News Publishers. Used by permission.

Scripture quotations marked (NIV) are taken from the Holy Bible, New International Version®, NIV® Copyright © 1973, 1978, 1984, 2011 by Biblica, Inc.™ Used by permission of Zondervan. All rights reserved worldwide. www.zondervan.com. The "NIV" and "New International Version" are trademarks registered in the United States Patent and Trademark Office by Biblica, Inc. ™

Scripture quotations marked KJV are from the Holy Bible, King James Version.

To order additional copies of this resource, write to Lifeway Resources Customer Service; 200 Powell Place, Suite 100, Brentwood, TN 37027-7707; order online at lifeway.com; fax 615.251.5933; phone toll free 800.458.2772; or email orderentry@lifeway.com.

Printed in the United States of America

Lifeway Women Bible Studies

Lifeway Resources

200 Powell Place, Suite 100

Brentwood, TN 37027-7707

Author is represented by Wolgemuth & Associates.

Contents

You version Bible (switch between versions)
message Bible

ABOUT THE AUTHOR

Jen Wilkin is an author and Bible teacher from Dallas, Texas. She has organized and led studies for women in home, church, and parachurch contexts. Her passion is to see others become articulate and committed followers of Christ, with a clear understanding of why they believe what they believe, grounded in the Word of God. Jen is the author of *Ten Words to Live By: Delighting in and Doing What God Commands, Women of the Word, None Like Him, In His Image,* and Bible studies exploring the Sermon on the Mount and the books of Genesis, Exodus, Hebrews, and 1 Peter. You can find her at jenwilkin.net.

FOREWORD: HOW SHOULD WE APPROACH GOD'S WORD?

OUR PURPOSE

The Bible study you are about to begin will teach you an important passage of the Bible in a way that will stay with you for years to come. It will challenge you to move beyond loving God with just your heart to loving Him with your mind. It will focus on answering the question, "What does the Bible say about God?" It will aid you in the worthy task of God-discovery.

You see, the Bible is not a book about self-discovery; it is a book about God-discovery. The Bible is God's declared intent to make Himself known to us. In learning about the character of God in Scripture, we *will* experience self-discovery, but it must not be the object of our study. The object must be God Himself.

This focus changes the way we study. We look first for what a passage can teach us about the character of God, allowing self-discovery to be the by-product of God-discovery. This is a much better approach because there can be no true knowledge of self apart from knowledge of God. So when I read the account of Jonah, I see first that God is just and faithful to His Word—He is faithful to proclaim His message to Nineveh no matter what. I see second that I, by contrast (and much like Jonah), am unjust to my fellow man and unfaithful to God's Word. Thus, knowledge of God leads to true knowledge of self, which leads to repentance and transformation. So are confirmed Paul's words in Romans 12:2 that we are transformed by the renewing of our minds.

Most of us are good at loving God with our hearts. We are good at employing our emotions in our pursuit of God. But the God who commands us to love with the totality of our hearts, souls, and strength also commands us to love Him with all of our minds. Because He only commands what He also enables His children to do, it must be possible for us to love Him well with our minds or He would not command it. I know you will bring your emotions to your study of God's Word, and that is good and right. But it is your mind I am jealous for. God intends for you to be a good student, renewing your mind and thus transforming your heart.

OUR PROCESS

Being a good student entails following good study habits. When we sit down to read, most of us like to read through a particular passage and then find a way to apply it to our everyday lives. We may read through an entire book of the Bible over a period of time, or we may jump around from place to place. I want to suggest a different approach, one that may not always yield immediate application, comfort, or peace, but one that builds over time a cumulative understanding of the message of Scripture.

READING IN CONTEXT AND REPETITIVELY

Imagine yourself receiving a letter in the mail. The envelope is handwritten, but you don't glance at the return address. Instead you tear open the envelope, flip to the second page, read two paragraphs near the bottom, and set the letter aside. Knowing that if someone bothered to send it to you, you should act on its contents in some way, you spend a few minutes trying to figure out how to respond to what the section you just read had to say. What are the odds you will be successful?

No one would read a letter this way. But this is precisely the way many of us read our Bibles. We skip past reading the "envelope"—*Who wrote this? To whom was it written? When was it written? Where was it written?*—and then try to determine the purpose of its contents from a portion of the whole. What if we took time to read the envelope? What if, after determining the context for its writing, we started at the beginning and read to the end? Wouldn't that make infinitely more sense?

In our study, we will take this approach to Scripture. We will begin by placing our text in its historical and cultural context. We will "read the envelope." Then we will read through the entire text so that we can better determine what it wants to say to us. We will read repetitively so that we might move through three critical stages of understanding: comprehension, interpretation, and application.

STAGE 1: COMPREHENSION

Remember the reading comprehension section on the SAT? Remember those long reading passages followed by questions to test your knowledge of what you had just read? The objective was to force you to read for detail. We are going to apply the same method to our study of God's Word. When we read for comprehension, we ask ourselves, *What does it say?* This is hard work. A person who *comprehends* the account of the six days of creation can tell you specifically what happened on each day. This is the first step toward being able to interpret and apply the story of creation to our lives.

STAGE 2: INTERPRETATION

While comprehension asks, *What does it say?*, interpretation asks, *What does it mean?* Once we have read a passage enough times to know what it says, we are ready to look into its meaning. A person who *interprets* the creation story can tell you why God created in a particular order or way. She is able to imply things from the text beyond what it says.

STAGE 3: APPLICATION

After doing the work to understand what the text says and what the text means, we are finally ready to ask, *How should it change me?* Here is where we draw on our God-centered perspective to ask three supporting questions:

- *What does this passage teach me about God?*

- *How does this aspect of God's character change my view of self?*

- *What should I do in response?*

A person who *applies* the creation story can tell us that because God creates in an orderly fashion, we, too, should live well-ordered lives. Knowledge of God gleaned through comprehension of the text and interpretation of its meaning can now be applied to my life in a way that challenges me to be different.

SOME GUIDELINES

It is vital to the learning process that you allow yourself to move through the three stages of understanding on your own, without the aid of commentaries or study notes. The first several times you read a passage, you will probably be confused. In our study together, not all the homework questions will have answers that are immediately clear to you. This is actually a good thing. If you are unsure of an answer, give it your best shot. Allow yourself to feel lost, to dwell in the "I don't know." It will make the moment of discovery stick. We'll also expand our understanding in the small-group discussion and teaching time.

Nobody likes to feel lost or confused, but it is an important step in the acquisition and retention of understanding. Because of this, I have a few guidelines to lay out for you as you go through this study.

1. **Avoid all commentaries** until *comprehension* and *interpretation* have been earnestly attempted on your own. In other words, wait to read commentaries

until after you have done the homework, attended small-group time, and listened to the teaching. And then, consult commentaries you can trust. Ask a pastor or Bible teacher at your church for suggested authors. I used the following commentaries in creating this study: *1, 2, and 3 John* by Karen Jobes, *The Epistles of John* by James Montgomery Boice, and *The MacArthur New Testament Commentary (Volume 31), 1-3 John* by John MacArthur.

2. For the purposes of this study, **get a Bible without study notes.** Come on, it's just too easy to look at them. You know I'm right.

3. Though commentaries are initially off-limits, here are some **tools you should use:**

- **Cross-references.** These are the Scripture references in the margin or at the bottom of the page in your Bible. They point you to other passages that deal with the same topic or theme.

- **An English dictionary** to look up unfamiliar words. A good online dictionary is *merriam-webster.com.*

- **Other translations of the Bible.** We will use the English Standard Version (ESV) as a starting point, but you can easily consult other versions online. I recommend the Christian Standard Bible (CSB), New International Version (NIV), New American Standard Version (NASB), and New King James Version (NKJV). Reading more than one translation can expand your understanding of the meaning of a passage. Note: a paraphrase, such as The Message, can be useful but should be regarded as a commentary rather than a translation. They are best consulted after careful study of an actual translation.

- **A printed copy of the text,** double-spaced, so you can mark repeated words, phrases, or ideas. A complete copy of 1, 2, 3 John is provided for you to mark at the back of this workbook.

STORING UP TREASURE

Approaching God's Word with a God-centered perspective, with context, and with care takes effort and commitment. It is study for the long-term. Some days your study may not move you emotionally or speak to an immediate need. You may not be able to apply a passage at all. But what if ten years from now, in a dark night of the soul, that passage suddenly opens up to you because of the work you have done today? Wouldn't your long-term investment be worth it? In Matthew 13 we see Jesus begin to teach in parables. He tells seven deceptively simple stories that left His disciples struggling for understanding—dwelling in the "I don't know," if you will. After the last parable, He turns to them and asks, "Have you understood all these things?" (v. 51a). Despite their apparent confusion, they answer out of their earnest desire with, "Yes" (v. 51b). Jesus tells them that their newfound understanding makes them "like the owner of a house who brings out of his storeroom new treasures as well as old" (v. 52, NIV).

A storeroom, as Jesus indicated, is a place for keeping valuables over a long period of time for use when needed. Faithful study of God's Word is a means for filling our spiritual storerooms with truth, so that in our hour of need we can bring forth both the old and the new as a source of rich provision. I pray that this study would be for you a source of much treasure and that you would labor well to obtain it.

Grace and peace,

Jen Wilkin

HOW TO USE THIS STUDY

This workbook is designed to be used in a specific way. The homework in the workbook will start you in the process of comprehension, interpretation, and application. However, it was designed to dovetail with small-group discussion time and the video teaching sessions. You can use the workbook by itself, but you are likely to find yourself with some unresolved questions. The video teaching sessions are intended to resolve most, if not all, of your unanswered questions from the homework and discussion time. You'll find detailed information for how to access the video teaching sessions that accompany this study on the card inserted in the back of your workbook. With this in mind, consider using the materials as follows:

You'll find detailed information for how to **ACCESS THE VIDEO TEACHING SESSIONS** that accompany this study on the card inserted in the back of your workbook.

- If you are going through the study **on your own**, first work through the homework, and then watch the corresponding video teaching for that week.

- If you are going through the study **in a group**, first do your homework, and then discuss the questions your group decides to cover. Then watch the video teaching. Some groups watch the teaching before they meet, which can also work if that format fits best for everyone. Group leaders, you'll find promotional materials and more tools to help you lead at **lifeway.com/abide**.

Note: For Week One, there is no homework. The study begins with a video introduction. You will find a Viewer Guide on pages 14–15 that you can use as you watch the introductory material.

ACKNOWLEDGMENT

I am deeply grateful to Jenni Hamm for her editorial help on this study. Her insights, attention to detail, and love for the Lord and His Word have been indispensable to me. She has graciously shared the load of this joyful burden and so fulfilled the law of Christ. She is a sweet friend and "fellow worker for the truth" (3 John 8).

HOW TO USE THE GROUP DISCUSSION GUIDE

At the end of each week's homework you will find a leader guide intended to help facilitate discussion in small groups. The group discussion guide includes questions to help group members compare what they have learned from their homework. These questions are either pulled directly from the homework, or they summarize a concept or theme that the homework covered. Each section covers content from a particular day of the homework, first asking group members to observe and then asking them to apply. The observation questions typically ask group members to report a finding or flesh out an interpretation. The application questions challenge them to move beyond intellectual understanding and to identify ways to live differently in light of what they have learned.

As a small group leader, you will want to review these questions before you meet with your group, thinking through your own answers, marking where they occur in the homework, and noting if there are any additional questions you might want to reference to help the flow of the discussion. These questions are suggestions only, intended to help you cover as much ground as you can in a forty-five-minute discussion time. They should not be seen as requirements or limitations, but as guidelines to help you prepare your group for the teaching time by allowing them to process collectively what they have learned during their homework.

As a facilitator of discussion rather than a teacher, you are allowed and encouraged to be a colearner with your group members. This means you yourself may not always feel confident of your answer to a given question, and that is perfectly OK. Because we are studying for the long-term, we are allowed to leave some questions partially answered or unresolved, trusting for clarity at a later time. In most cases, the video teaching time should address any lingering questions that are not resolved in the homework or the small-group discussion time.

INTRODUCTION I YOU'VE GOT MAIL

Who wrote 1, 2, and 3 John?

To whom were they written?

When were they written?

To access the video teaching sessions, use the instructions in the back of your workbook.

In what style were they written?

What are the central themes of the letters?

Week
Two

A CREDIBLE WITNESS

As we discussed in our introduction, repetitive reading helps you learn and retain what a book of the Bible has to say. Hopefully, you have taken the opportunity to read through 1, 2, and 3 John already to get a high-level view of what we will be studying. Each week before you begin your study, make it your goal to read through all three letters. As you read, think about what you learned about John the disciple in the introductory lesson. Think about the five questions we answered about the letters.

Your weekly homework will focus in on a particular passage to see what it has to say and how it fits into the greater context of the message. The homework is designed to help you take a closer look at what you are reading. Beginning in Week Six, you'll choose a passage from the text that has been meaningful to you, one that has already had an impact on your relationships or your perspective, and you'll begin to commit it to memory.

On page 176 of your workbook you will find a printed copy of 1, 2, and 3 John. You will need it to complete your homework each week. You will also need a set of colored pens or pencils. We will be marking key words or phrases, as well as looking up some words in the dictionary or thesaurus. A good online dictionary is merriam-webster.com.

Not all the homework questions will have answers that are immediately clear to you. If you are unsure of an answer, give it your best shot. We'll expand our understanding in the small group discussion and teaching time.

Let's get started.

Day One

READ 1 JOHN 1:1–2:2.

1. In two to three sentences, summarize the main ideas of the passage.

2. Remember our premise that the Bible is a book about God? We want to know Him better at the end of our study. At the beginning of each week's homework, we'll take time to read through the text and note everything we learn about God. Your notes might center on one member of the Trinity or the Godhead as a whole. Read asking these questions:

    ☐ What is He like?

    ☐ What has He done? What is He doing? What will He do?

    ☐ What pleases Him? What displeases Him?

    Do this now for 1 John 1:1–2:2. Here are some examples to get you started.

    > God (Jesus) is "from the beginning" (1:1).
    >
    > Jesus was physically present among us (1:1).
    >
    > Jesus is life (1:2).

3. In two places in our passage for this week, John tells his audience why he is writing to them. As you read through the passage, note the two verses and the reason John gives for writing.

VERSE	REASON

How are these two reasons related to each other?

NOW LOOK MORE CLOSELY AT 1 JOHN 1:1-4.

4. The word *proclaim* occurs twice. Specifically, what does John proclaim in this passage?

5. In your copy of the text, underline in pink the phrase "from the beginning" (v. 1). Draw a tiny clock face above it. What or who does John mean by "That which was from the beginning" (v. 1)? Compare with the Gospel of John 1:1-5,14.

6. In your copy of the text, underline each occurrence of the word *life* in green.

   Who or what is the "life"? _____

7. Look up the Gospel of John 17:3. Note Jesus's definition of eternal life. How does it expand your understanding of 1 John 1:1-4?

8. **APPLY:** Based on the Gospel of John 17:3, when does eternal life begin?

   How has knowing "the only true God, and Jesus Christ whom [He has] sent" (John 17:3) been life-giving for you? Think of specific areas of your life that have been redeemed from death.

Day Two

NOW LOOK BACK AT 1 JOHN 1:1-4.

9. John repeats twice that the life "was made manifest" (v. 2). Look up the word *manifest* in a dictionary or thesaurus. Write a definition for it that best fits with the way it is used in the passage. Note any synonyms listed.

MANIFEST

10. Reread 1 John 1:1-2, with your definition in mind. How does it add to your understanding of what John is saying?

11. Circle each time John uses the words *heard*, *seen*, or *touched*. Why do you think John expresses himself this way? What does he want to communicate to his readers?

12. Look up the following passages. Read through each one carefully, looking for John's presence in the narrative. For each passage, note what of significance John *saw*, *heard*, or *touched*.

Luke 5:1-11	
Luke 8:40-56	
Luke 9:28-36	
Gospel of John 20:1-9	
Luke 24:36-40	

13. **APPLY:** John was uniquely qualified to testify about the Word of Life. He was an eyewitness to the life of the God-Man, Jesus. No one alive today can make that claim. Consider, though: In what ways are you qualified to testify concerning the Word of Life? How have you witnessed the Word of Life at work?

Day Three

NOW READ THROUGH THE END OF CHAPTER 1.

14. Underline every occurrence of the word *fellowship* in chapter 1 in red.

15. Look up the word *fellowship* in a dictionary or thesaurus. Based on what you find, write a definition that best fits the way the word is used in the passage.

FELLOWSHIP

16. According to John, what enables us to have fellowship with God and each other? What hinders us? Note what you find.

17. In 1 John 1:5-10, what pair of opposites does John use to make his point about fellowship?

_____ and _____

18. How is light an accurate metaphor for God? List some thoughts.

How is darkness an accurate metaphor for sin?

19. <mark>APPLY:</mark> Think about light, darkness, and fellowship as described in 1 John 1:5-10. What keeps us from having deep, real fellowship with our fellow Christians? Why do we settle for surface relationships?

What attitudes or actions would help us to move beyond surface relationships to authentic Christian fellowship with one another?

Day Four

NOW LOOK AT 1 JOHN 1:5-10.

20. Look at verses 8 and 10. Why might someone claim to be without sin?

21. How would saying that we have not sinned make God a liar? Give a specific Scripture reference to back up your answer, if you can.

22. Look at verse 9. Look up the word *confess* in a dictionary or thesaurus. Based on what you find, write a definition that best fits the way the word is used in the passage.

CONFESS

23. If God already knows our sins, why is confession necessary?

24. In verse 9, what two adjectives are used to describe the God who forgives our sins?

_____ and _____

How is God's forgiveness of our sins an act of *faithfulness* on His part?

How is God's forgiveness of our sins an act of *justice* on His part?

25. **APPLY:** Why are we slow to confess our sins to God? To each other?

What lies do we tell ourselves when we avoid confessing our offenses? How does unconfessed sin break Christian fellowship?

Day Five

CONCLUDE BY READING 1 JOHN 2:1-2.

26. Note how John addresses his readers in 1 John 2:1. What does his choice of address reveal about his motive for writing to them?

27. Two words are used to describe Jesus's role in dealing with our sin. With the help of a dictionary or thesaurus, write a definition for each.

ADVOCATE (noun)

PROPITIATION

(Hint: look up propitiate and modify the definition to a noun form, or look up propitiatory in the thesaurus.)

28. Paraphrasing a verse or passage (rewriting it in our own words) can help us to focus on its meaning. It is a useful study tool for a student of the Word. We will use it often in this study. Based on your definitions on the previous page, rewrite verses 1-2 in your own words.

29. <mark>APPLY:</mark> Why is it significant that Christ is both your Advocate and your Propitiation? How do these dual truths cause you to worship and spur you on toward holiness?

Wrap-up

What aspect of God's character has this week's passage of 1 John shown you more clearly? *(Note: Each week we will end our homework by focusing on what the text has revealed about God. A list of God's attributes can be found in the back of your workbook on pages 186–187 to help you think through your answer to the wrap-up questions.)*

Fill in the following statement:

Knowing that God is _____ shows me that I am _____.

What one step can you take this week to better live in light of this truth?

1. OBSERVE: (question 7, p. 20) Look up the Gospel of John 17:3. Note Jesus's definition of eternal life. How does it expand your understanding of 1 John 1:1-4?

APPLY: (question 8, p. 20) Based on the Gospel of John 17:3, when does eternal life begin?

How has knowing "the only true God, and Jesus Christ whom [He has] sent" (John 17:3) been life-giving for you? Think of specific areas of your life that have been redeemed from death.

2. OBSERVE: (question 16, p. 23) According to John, what enables us to have fellowship with God and each other? What hinders us?

APPLY: (question 19, p. 24) Think about light, darkness, and fellowship as described in 1 John 1:5-10. What keeps us from having deep, real fellowship with our fellow Christians? Why do we settle for surface relationships?

What attitudes or actions would help us to move beyond surface relationships to authentic Christian fellowship with one another?

3. OBSERVE: (question 23, p. 25) If God already knows our sins, why is confession necessary?

APPLY: (question 25, p. 26) Why are we slow to confess our sins to God? To each other?

What lies do we tell ourselves when we avoid confessing our offenses? How does unconfessed sin break Christian fellowship?

4. OBSERVE: (question 26, p. 27) Note how John addresses his readers in 1 John 2:1. What does his choice of address reveal about his motive for writing to them?

APPLY: (question 29, p. 28) Why is it significant that Christ is both your Advocate and your Propitiation? How do these dual truths cause you to worship and spur you on toward holiness?

5. WRAP-UP: (p. 29) What aspect of God's character has this week's passage of 1 John shown you more clearly?

Fill in the following statement:

Knowing that God is _____ *shows me that I am* _____.

What one step can you take this week to better live in light of this truth?

WEEK TWO | VIEWER GUIDE NOTES

To access the video teaching sessions, use the instructions in the back of your workbook.

Week Three

THE TESTS OF RIGHTEOUSNESS AND LOVE

Day One

Remember to take time this week to read through 1, 2, and 3 John from beginning to end. You can read it in one sitting or break it out across your week. Once you have completed your read-through, note one new observation that became clear to you.

READ THIS WEEK'S SECTION OF TEXT: 1 JOHN 2:3-17.

1. What does this passage teach us about God? Note your observations.

2. What do you think John wants to communicate in 1 John 2:3-17? What theme does he continue from the previous section?

3. Summarize this section of the text in two to three sentences.

NOW READ 1 JOHN 2:3-14.

4. In your copy of the text, continue to underline in pink the phrase *from the beginning* (v. 1). Draw a tiny clock face above it. Next, mark each occurrence of the word *know* with a blue pencil. John uses the word *know* in more than one way, sometimes within the same sentence. Above each occurrence of the word, write a synonym or brief definition for how you think the word is used in that particular spot.

Day Two

NOW READ 1 JOHN 2:3-6—THE TEST OF RIGHTEOUSNESS.

5. John offers a test in 1 John 2:3-6 for proving that we truly know "Jesus Christ, the righteous" (v. 1). What is the test?

6. Why is it a lie to claim to know God without obeying Him?

7. Look up Matthew 7:21-23. How does Jesus use the concept of "knowing" in this passage? What does He mean to communicate by His use of the term?

8. Now look back at Matthew 7:15-20. Note the context of Jesus's remarks about whom He "knows." To whom will Jesus say, "I never knew you" (v. 15)?

Now connect the words of Jesus in Matthew 7:15-20 to 1 John 2:3-6. What would both Jesus and John say is one test we can use to discern whether someone's profession of faith is genuine?

9. How does keeping God's Word *perfect* (verb) His love in us (1 John 2:5)?
    Does John mean we will become perfect? Why or why not?

10. **APPLY:** Think about your own life. Do you "walk in the same way in which
    he walked" (v. 6)? Think about what you know about the story of Jesus's
    "walk" on earth. Ask God to show you specific ways you can walk more as
    Jesus walked. Write them below as you pray over each of them.

Day Three

READ 1 JOHN 2:7-11—THE TEST OF LOVE.

11. John has discussed obeying God's commandments in general, but now he gets more specific. Mark every occurrence of the word *commandment(s)* in verses 3-11 with a gray underline. You may also want to draw a small icon of the Ten Commandments above it. What is the new command that is also an old command, that he wants his readers to obey? Look up the following verses to help you with your answer.

    Leviticus 19:18

    Matthew 22:34-40

    John 13:34-35

12. Look at 1 John 2:8. How is the new commandment "true in him" (Jesus) and in us? Look up the following verses and note how each adds to your understanding.

    Gospel of John 15:12-13

    1 John 3:16

13. In 1 John 2:8-11, John returns to the contrasting images of light and darkness. What new pair of contrasting terms does he also introduce?

_____ and _____

John uses the term *agape* for *love*. It is defined as *an intelligent, purposeful attitude of esteem and devotion; a selfless, purposeful, outgoing attitude that desires to do good to the one loved.*[1] In light of this definition, how would you define *hate*?

14. According to 1 John 2:9-11, how can we test who is "in the light"?

15. **APPLY:** Two believing women in your small group hold radically different political views. They are constantly in conflict. How would you counsel them to live in light of 1 John 2:9-11?

Think about your own relationships. Is there anyone you should love with a more "intelligent, purposeful attitude of esteem and devotion"? Stop and pray that God would bring someone to mind. Write their name below. Ask Him to show you tangible ways to love them.

1. Kenneth Wuest, *Kenneth Wuest's Word Studies in the Greek New Testament* (Grand Rapids, Michigan: Wm. B. Eerdmans Publishing Co,. 1975), Vol. III Bypaths, 111–113.

Day Four

NOW READ 1 JOHN 2:12-14.

16. Fill in the chart.

I write to you . . .	. . . because . . .	. . . and because . . .
children	v. 12	v. 13
fathers	v. 13	v. 14
young men	v. 13	v. 14

17. Why do you think John addresses these three groups specifically? Does he mean these terms literally or figuratively?

18. Within the context of a community of believers, who would be a "child"? A "young man"? A "father"?

How does this change your reading of verses 12-14?

19. **APPLY:** These poetic verses give beautiful assurances of our identity in Christ. Which one do you find particularly comforting? Why?

Day Five

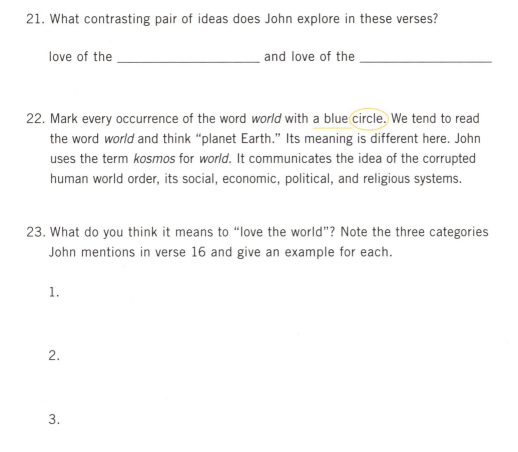

READ 1 JOHN 2:15-17.

20. What warning does John give in these verses? Summarize his thoughts.

21. What contrasting pair of ideas does John explore in these verses?

love of the _____ and love of the _____

22. Mark every occurrence of the word *world* with a blue circle. We tend to read the word *world* and think "planet Earth." Its meaning is different here. John uses the term *kosmos* for *world*. It communicates the idea of the corrupted human world order, its social, economic, political, and religious systems.

23. What do you think it means to "love the world"? Note the three categories John mentions in verse 16 and give an example for each.

1.

2.

3.

24. Based on your answer to the previous question, what would be the opposite of loving the world? Give some examples.

25. **APPLY:** How can we know if we are too enamored with the world? What warning signs should we look for?

What is a particular aspect of this world that you are too enamored with? What advice would John give you to redirect your affections?

Wrap-up

What aspect of God's character has this week's passage of 1 John shown you more clearly?

Fill in the following statement:

Knowing that God is _____ shows me that I am _____.

What one step can you take this week to better live in light of this truth?

1. OBSERVE: (question 9, p. 38) How does keeping God's word *perfect* (verb) His love in us (1 John 2:5)? Does John mean we will become perfect? Why or why not?

APPLY: (question 10, p. 38) Think about your own life. Do you "walk in the same way in which he walked" (v. 6)? Think about what you know about the story of Jesus's "walk" on earth. Ask God to show you specific ways you can walk more as Jesus walked. Write them as you pray over each of them.

2. OBSERVE: (question 14, p. 40) According to 1 John 2:9-11, how can we test who is "in the light"?

APPLY: (question 15, p. 40) Two believing women in your small group hold radically different political views. They are constantly in conflict. How would you counsel them to live in light of 1 John 2:9-11?

3. OBSERVE: (question 18, p. 42) Within the context of a community of believers, who would be a "child"? a "young man"? a "father"?

How does this change your reading of 1 John 2:12-14?

APPLY: (question 19, p. 42) These poetic verses give beautiful assurances of our identity in Christ. Which one do you find particularly comforting? Why?

4. **OBSERVE:** (question 20, p. 43) What warning does John give in these verses? Summarize his thoughts.

APPLY: (question 25, p. 44) How can we know if we are too enamored with the world? What warning signs should we look for?

What is a particular aspect of this world that you are too enamored with? What advice would John give you to redirect your affections?

5. **WRAP-UP:** (p. 45) What aspect of God's character has this week's passage of 1 John shown you more clearly?

Fill in the following statement:

Knowing that God is _____ *shows me that I am* _____.

What one step can you take this week to better live in light of this truth?

WEEK THREE | VIEWER GUIDE NOTES

To access the video teaching sessions, use the instructions in the back of your workbook.

1 JOHN 2:18-29

Week Four

THE TEST OF TRUTH, THE CALL TO ABIDE

Day One

Remember to take time this week to read through 1, 2, and 3 John from beginning to end. Once you have completed your read-through, note one new observation that became clear to you.

READ THIS WEEK'S SECTION OF TEXT: 1 JOHN 2:18-29.

1. Summarize this section of the text in two to three sentences.

2. Continue your annotating as in previous weeks. Read through the text several times, marking two key words each time you read. Focus on how the words shape the meaning of 1 John.

   ☐ Mark the word *know/known* in blue. Above it, note its meaning in the context of the sentence.

   ☐ Mark the phrase *from the beginning* (v. 1) with an underline in pink. Draw a tiny clock face above it.

   ☐ Mark with a red devil head (I draw a circle with two horns) the word *antichrist(s)* and the related pronouns (*they/those*).

3. What does this passage teach us about God? Note your observations.

NOW LOOK AT 1 JOHN 2:18-25—THE TEST OF TRUTH.

4. John's letter was written more than nineteen hundred years ago. What do you think he means by "it is the last hour" (v. 18)? Was he wrong to think this? Give your best answer. We will discuss it further in the teaching time.

5. Look at verse 19. Who do you think John means by those who "went out from us"? Does someone "go out from us" when they leave our church? Our denomination? The Christian faith?

6. Is John indicating that those who "went out from us" are believers who abandoned their faith? Explain your answer. Give a Scripture to support it if you can.

7. What does John mean by "what you heard from the beginning" (vv. 24-25)?

8. **APPLY:** What are some types of false teaching that are prevalent today? With whom are they popular? What makes these teachings attractive?

   Do false teachers only harm unbelievers? What impact do they have on believers?

Day Two

LOOK AT 1 JOHN 2:26-27.

9. What is "the anointing that you received from him" (v. 27)? Look up Acts 2:1-4 to help with your answer.

10. Is John saying that we do not need other people to instruct us about truth? Look up Ephesians 4:11-13 to help with your answer. Based on what you find there, explain what you think John means.

11. Read back through verses 18-27. As you read, mark every variation of the words *true/truth/confess* in orange. Mark every variation of the words *lie/liar/deny/deceive/does not confess/error* in purple.

12. Is the contrasting idea of truth and lies a new one? Skim back through 1:1–2:17 and mark the earlier occurrences of this theme as you did in this week's portion of the text.

13. As he does in his epistles, John heavily emphasizes the theme of truth versus deception in his Gospel. Look up the following verses from the Gospel of John and note what you learn about the source of truth.

John 8:44

John 14:6

John 15:26

John 16:13

John 17:17

John 18:37

14. **APPLY:** Based on the previous verses, what steps can we take to better arm ourselves with truth and guard against falling prey to a false teacher? List several ideas.

Have you or someone you know ever been caught up in the teachings of a false teacher? How did the situation resolve itself?

Day Three

READ 1 JOHN 2:18-27 TOGETHER WITH 1 JOHN 4:1-6.

15. John's discussion of false teachers begins in 1 John 2:18-27 and is reinforced in 1 John 4:1-6. We will consider them together this week and will revisit 4:1-6 again in Week Six. According to these two parallel passages, how can we know or test if someone is an antichrist (false teacher)?

2:19

2:22-23

4:2-3

16. What will protect us from being swayed by the teachings of antichrist?

2:20,27

2:24

4:5-6

17. Based on your reading of these passages, is there only one antichrist? Look ahead to 2 John 7 to help with your answer.

18. **APPLY:** A friend has become very drawn to the teachings of a false teacher who teaches that Jesus is just one of many ways to God. When questioned, she acknowledges the problem, but responds that "the Holy Spirit is so evidently present when he teaches." How would you lovingly point her toward recognizing the false teacher as such?

Day Four

NOW LOOK AT 1 JOHN 2:28.

19. Look back through all of chapter 2, marking each occurrence of the word *abide* with a yellow highlighter.

20. What do you think John means by this term? Look up the word *abide* in a dictionary or thesaurus. Check out some other translations of 1 John 2 to see what other words are used to translate the idea of *abide*. Write some synonyms for the word.

ABIDE

21. Read the verse printed below.
    Jesus answered and said unto him, If a man love me, he will keep my words: and my Father will love him, and we will come unto him, and make our abode with him.
    John 14:23 (KJV)

    Now look up John 14:23 in another translation, like the ESV or the CSB. What word is used in place of *abode*? _____

22. **APPLY:** Think about the connotations of the word *home*. How does the knowledge that the Godhead makes His home with those who love Him encourage you to abide in Him?

Day Five

LOOK AGAIN AT 1 JOHN 2:28.

23. John says those who abide in Christ will "have confidence and not shrink from him in shame at his coming." Look up the word *confidence* in a dictionary or thesaurus and write a definition for it that fits the way it is used in the passage.

CONFIDENCE	

24. Why can believers have confidence when Christ comes in judgment? Look up the following verses to help with your answer.

Ephesians 5:27

Colossians 1:22

1 Thessalonians 3:13

1 Thessalonians 5:23

25. Now look up the Gospel of John 15:1-11. Answer the following questions.

Who is speaking? _____ To whom? _____

What familiar word from 1 John is repeated again and again in this passage? _____

How many times does it occur? _____

Note every benefit and instruction associated with this word.

In light of your answers, why do you think the apostle John loves to speak of "abiding" in his letters to the early church?

26. One of my favorite hymns is "Abide with Me" by Henry F. Lyte. Below are the lyrics. If you'd like, find a version of the hymn on YouTube® or an online hymnal to hear how it sounds. Read through the lyrics and reflect on how they play on the themes of 1 John: darkness and light, little children, the world, antichrist (enemies of Christ), abiding, and the victory of the cross. Mark them as you find them in the lyrics:

Abide with me; fast falls the eventide;
the darkness deepens; Lord, with me abide.
When other helpers fail and comforts flee,
Help of the helpless, O abide with me.

Swift to its close ebbs out life's little day;
earth's joys grow dim; its glories pass away;
change and decay in all around I see;
O thou who changest not, abide with me.

I need thy presence every passing hour.

What but thy grace can foil the tempter's power?

Who, like Thyself, my guide and stay can be?

Through cloud and sunshine, O, abide with me.

I fear no foe, with thee at hand to bless;

ills have no weight, and tears not bitterness.

Where is death's sting? Where, grave, thy victory?

I triumph still, if thou abide with me.

Hold thou thy cross before my closing eyes;

shine through the gloom and point me to the skies.

Heaven's morning breaks, and earth's vain shadows flee;

in life, in death, O Lord, abide with me.[1]

27. **APPLY:** What are two specific ways you can abide in the truth and guard yourself against straying into error this week? What are two specific difficult circumstances in which you could ask the Lord to abide with you?

---

1. Henry F. Lyte "Abide with Me," 1847.

Wrap-up

What aspect of God's character has this week's passage of 1 John shown you more clearly?

Fill in the following statement:

Knowing that God is _____ shows me that I am _____.

What one step can you take this week to better live in light of this truth?

1. OBSERVE: (question 5, p. 53) Look at verse 19. Who do you think John means by those who "went out from us"? Does someone "go out from us" when they leave our church? Our denomination? The Christian faith?

APPLY: (question 8, p. 53) What are some types of false teaching that are prevalent today? With whom are they popular? What makes these teachings attractive?

Do false teachers only harm unbelievers? What impact do they have on believers?

2. OBSERVE: (question 10, p. 54) Is John saying that we do not need other people to instruct us about truth? Look up Ephesians 4:11-13 to help with your answer. Based on what you find there, explain what you think John means.

APPLY: (question 14, p. 55) Based on the previous verses, what steps can we take to better arm ourselves with truth and guard against falling prey to a false teacher? List several ideas.

Have you or someone you know ever been caught up in the teachings of a false teacher? How did the situation resolve itself?

3. OBSERVE: (question 16, p. 56) What will protect us from being swayed by the teachings of antichrist?

APPLY: (question 18, p. 57) A friend has become very drawn to the teachings of a false teacher who teaches that Jesus is just one of many ways to God. When questioned, she acknowledges the problem, but responds that "the Holy Spirit is so evidently present when he teaches." How would you lovingly point her toward recognizing the false teacher as such?

4. **OBSERVE:** (question 25, p. 60) In light of the answers you listed in the first part of question 25, why do you think the apostle John loves to speak of "abiding" in his letters to the early church?

APPLY: (question 27, p. 61) What are two specific ways you can abide in the truth and guard yourself against straying into error this week? What are two specific difficult circumstances in which you could ask the Lord to abide with you?

5. **WRAP-UP:** (p. 62) What aspect of God's character has this week's passage of 1 John shown you more clearly?

Fill in the following statement:

Knowing that God is _____ *shows me that I am* _____.

What one step can you take this week to better live in light of this truth?

WEEK FOUR | VIEWER GUIDE NOTES

To access the video teaching sessions, use the instructions in the back of your workbook.

Week
Five

PRACTICE RIGHTEOUSNESS, PURSUE LOVE, POSSESS ASSURANCE

Day One

Remember to take some time this week to read through 1, 2, and 3 John from beginning to end. Once you have completed your read-through, note one new observation that became clear to you:

READ THIS WEEK'S SECTION OF TEXT: 1 JOHN 2:29–3:24.

In the previous weeks we have examined the three tests of genuine faith that John gave to his "little children."

The test of righteousness	Do we show we know God by obeying His commands?
The test of love	Do we show we know God by loving our brother?
The test of truth	Do we show we know God by confessing that Jesus is the Christ?

This week we will examine what it means to be a part of God's family, to be "called children of God." How does a member of God's family regard sin? How does he regard his brother?

1. Summarize this section of the text in two to three sentences.

2. Continue your annotating as in previous weeks. Read through the text several times, marking two key words each time you read. Focus on how the words shape the meaning of 1 John.

- ☐ Mark the phrase *from the beginning* (v. 1) in pink. Draw a tiny clock face above it.

- ☐ Mark the word *life/lives* in green.

- ☐ Mark the word *know/known* in blue. Above it, note its meaning in the context of the sentence.

- ☐ Mark the words *true/truth* in orange.

- ☐ Mark every occurrence of the word *world* with a blue circle.

- ☐ Highlight the word *abide* in yellow.

- ☐ Mark every occurrence of the word *commandment(s)* with a gray underline. You may also want to draw a small icon of the Ten Commandments above it.

- ☐ Mark with a red devil head the words *devil/evil one*.

3. What does this passage teach us about God? Note your observations.

Day Two

READ THROUGH 1 JOHN 2:28–3:18.

4. Circle each occurrence of the phrase *born of God/him* in green.

5. If you are born of someone, what is your natural relationship to that person? You are his or her _____.

6. Mark every occurrence of the word *children* by circling it in red.

7. In the space below, note everything you learn that should characterize those "born of God" or the "children of God."

8. **APPLY:** How is the parent-child relationship an appropriate illustration for God's relationship with those He saves?

    Belong
    Behave
    Become like Christ.

    How have you experienced the fatherhood of God personally? Write your thoughts.

Day Three

READ 1 JOHN 3:2-3.

9. In what ways do you think we will be like Christ "when he appears"? Look up the following verses to add to your understanding.

    1 Corinthians 15:42-49

    Ephesians 4:17-24

    Philippians 3:20-21

TAKE A CLOSER LOOK AT 1 JOHN 3:4-10.

10. Compare 3:4 and 3:7. What new pair of contrasting terms does John give us?

    _____ and _____

11. Look up the term *lawless* in a dictionary or thesaurus. Write a definition for it that fits with the way it is used in the passage.

    LAWLESS

lawless person - breaks, violates, disobeys, transgresses the law.

12. Why do you think John says that "sin is lawlessness" in verse 4?

13. Look back at 1 John 2:3-6. How does what John says in this earlier passage reinforce his claim that sin should be defined as lawlessness?

14. Now read Psalm 119:97. What was the psalmist's attitude toward God's law/commands/precepts/testimony?

    What action resulted from his attitude?

15. In 1 John 3:9, John says those born of God cannot keep on sinning. How can this be so? Is John saying that believers cease sinning altogether, or is he making a different point? Look up the word *practice* (verb) in a dictionary or thesaurus and write a definition for it that best fits the way it is used in the text.

PRACTICE

Now read through verses 4-10, marking every occurrence of the word *practice(s)* with a black underline. What kind of sinning is John saying we will stop committing as children born of God?

16. **APPLY:** What are some persistent or habitual sins that people commit? List some below.

idols,
judgemental thoughts,
impatience,
sharp words, tone

Can a person battle one of these sins and still be a Christian? Explain your answer.

Is there a persistent sin that you battle personally? How can you have assurance that you are a Christian, even though that particular sin persists?

judgemental thoughts
sharp words + tone

Day Four

NOW LOOK MORE CLOSELY AT 1 JOHN 3:10-18.

17. Mark every occurrence of the word *brother* by circling it in orange. Look back through chapters 1 and 2 and mark any previous occurrences you find.

18. Think about the context of what John is saying. If, being born of God, you are a child of God, then who are your brothers? Circle your answer.

my natural-born siblings
other believers
anyone in my sphere of influence

19. John uses the story of Cain and Abel to illustrate brotherly relations at their worst. Read the story in Genesis 4:1-16. What do you notice about Cain's attitude toward God? God's attitude toward Cain?

20. What pair of contrasting terms does John use in 3:11-18?

_____ and _____

21. Look back at your Week Three homework (p. 40) and Viewer Guide notes (p. 48) and fill in the definitions for *love* and *hate*.

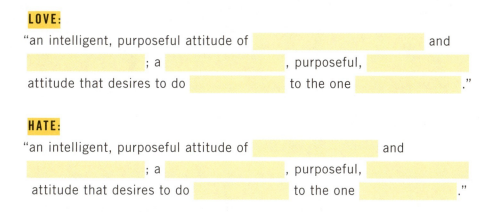

LOVE:

"an intelligent, purposeful attitude of ⬛⬛⬛ and ⬛⬛⬛ ; a ⬛⬛⬛ , purposeful, ⬛⬛⬛ attitude that desires to do ⬛⬛⬛ to the one ⬛⬛⬛ ."

HATE:

"an intelligent, purposeful attitude of ⬛⬛⬛ and ⬛⬛⬛ ; a ⬛⬛⬛ , purposeful, ⬛⬛⬛ attitude that desires to do ⬛⬛⬛ to the one ⬛⬛⬛ ."

22. Now mark each occurrence of the word *love* with a red heart and each occurrence of the word *hate* with a purple X in verses 11-18.

23. What do we know is true of us if we love our fellow believers (v. 14?)

    What do we know is true of us if we hate our fellow believers (vv. 14-15)?

24. In what way are we murderers if we hate our fellow believers? What does refusing to love someone have in common with murder?

25. In each of the verses below, note how John says we can tell genuine love from fake love.

Verse 16

Verse 17

Verse 18

26. **APPLY:** Has a fellow believer ever shown you the kind of sacrificial love described in 1 John 3:16-18? Describe that time.

Has the Lord brought to mind a fellow believer to whom you could show sacrificial love? How might you demonstrate openheartedness toward someone in need this week?

♡ sacrificially especially those that are more difficult to love.

Day Five

READ 1 JOHN 3:19-24.

27. This passage reiterates earlier themes John has introduced. How do his words in verses 19-24 increase your understanding about:

   ☐ Our confidence before God (see also 2:28)

   ☐ Keeping His commandments (see also 2:3-6)

   ☐ Abiding (see also 2:24-27)

28. What do you think John means by "God is greater than our heart, and he knows everything"? How should that thought "reassure our heart" (vv. 19-20)?

   Psalm 139

   God is greater than our ♡, + knoweth all things. *Isaiah 55:8-9*

   There are ∅ suprises to God.

29. Is John suggesting in verse 22 that our obedience to God will result in Him granting us whatever we ask? Is he saying we can earn God's favor through obedience? Explain your answer.

30. **APPLY:** What persistent sin or past failure is your heart most likely to condemn you on an ongoing basis? How do verses 19-24 offer you reassurance before God?

Wrap-up

What aspect of God's character has this week's passage of 1 John shown you more clearly?

Fill in the following statement:

*Knowing that God is _____ shows me
that I am _____.*

What one step can you take this week to better live in light of this truth?

WEEK FIVE | GROUP DISCUSSION

1. OBSERVE: (question 7, p. 72) Note everything you learn that should characterize those "born of God" or the "children of God."

APPLY: (question 8, p. 72) How is the parent-child relationship an appropriate illustration for God's relationship with those He saves? How have you experienced the fatherhood of God personally? Write your thoughts.

2. OBSERVE: (question 15, p. 74) In 1 John 3:9, John says those born of God cannot keep on sinning. How can this be so? Is John saying that believers cease sinning altogether, or is he making a different point?

APPLY: (question 16, p. 75) What are some persistent or habitual sins that people commit?

Can a person battle one of these sins and still be a Christian? Explain your answer.

Is there a persistent sin that you battle personally? How can you have assurance that you are a Christian, even though that particular sin persists?

3. OBSERVE: (question 23, p. 77) What do we know is true of us if we love our fellow believers (v. 14)?

What do we know is true of us if we hate our fellow believers (vv. 14-15)?

APPLY: (question 26, p. 78) Has a fellow believer ever shown you the kind of sacrificial love described in 1 John 3:16-18? Describe that time.

Has the Lord brought to mind a fellow believer to whom you could show sacrificial love? How might you demonstrate openheartedness toward someone in need this week?

4. OBSERVE: (question 29, p. 79) Is John suggesting in verse 22 that our obedience to God will result in Him granting us whatever we ask? Is he saying we can earn God's favor through obedience? Explain your answer.

APPLY: (question 30, p. 80) What persistent sin or past failure is your heart most likely to condemn you on an ongoing basis? How do verses 19-24 offer you reassurance before God?

5. WRAP-UP: (p. 81) What aspect of God's character has this week's passage of 1 John shown you more clearly?

Fill in the following statement:

Knowing that God is _____ *shows me that I am* _____.

What one step can you take this week to better live in light of this truth?

WEEK FIVE | VIEWER GUIDE NOTES

To access the video teaching sessions, use the instructions in the back of your workbook.

Week
Six

TRUTH
AND ERROR;
GOD IS LOVE

Day One

Remember to take time this week to read through 1, 2, and 3 John from beginning to end. Choose a passage from the text that has been meaningful to you, one that has already had an impact on your relationships or your perspective. Spend some time committing the beginning of your chosen passage to memory.

READ THIS WEEK'S SECTION OF TEXT: 1 JOHN 4:1-21.

Last week we considered what it means to be a part of God's family, to be "called children of God." We learned that God abides in us and we abide in Him. John concluded last week's portion of the text with the reassurance that the Spirit of God has given us proof of our sonship.

1. Summarize this section of the text in two to three sentences.

2. Continue your annotating as in previous weeks. Read through the text several times, marking two key words each time you read. Focus on how the words shape the meaning of 1 John.

    ☐ Mark the word *life/live* in green.

    ☐ Circle each occurrence of the phrase *born of God/him* in green.

    ☐ Mark the word *know/known* in blue. Above it, note its meaning in the context of the sentence.

    ☐ Highlight the word *abide* in yellow.

    ☐ Mark every occurrence of the word *children* by circling it in red.

    ☐ Mark every occurrence of the word *practice(s)* with a black underline.

- ☐ Mark every occurrence of the word *brother* by circling it in orange.

- ☐ Mark each occurrence of the word *love* with a red heart and each occurrence of the word *hate* with a purple X.

- ☐ Mark every occurrence of the word *world* with a blue circle.

- ☐ Mark every occurrence of the words *true/truth/confess* in orange. Mark every occurrence of the words *lie/liar/deny/deceive/does not confess/error* in purple.

- ☐ Mark every occurrence of the word *commandment(s)* with a gray underline. You may also want to draw a small icon of the Ten Commandments above it.

- ☐ Mark the words *false prophets/antichrist* and the related pronouns (*they*) with a red devil head.

3. What does this passage teach us about God? Note your observations.

NOW LOOK AT 1 JOHN 4:1-6.

4. How does verse 1 flow naturally out of the concluding verse we covered last week?

5. What two contrasting ideas does John present in verses 1-6, especially verse 6?

the Spirit of _____ and the spirit of _____

6. Compare 1 John 4:5 with 1 John 3:13. Also look up the Gospel of John 15:18-19. What do these verses teach you about how the "world" responds to those who abide in God? How does this impact how believers discern between truth and error?

7. **APPLY:** Think about your own life. Have you experienced hatred from the world because you *know* God? Give an example.

Think of some instances when you have sought to avoid the world's hatred of you in any way by disguising or downplaying your relationship with God. Write them below.

What steps do you need to take to walk as a child of God, regardless of the world's opinion of you?

Reminds me of Texas :

Philippians 4:13

Day Two

NOW LOOK AT 1 JOHN 4:7-8.

8. In verse 7, the love that "is from God" is *agape* love, the selfless love we have defined in previous weeks, the kind perfectly displayed by Christ.

    Think back over our previous discussions of this term. How is human love different from God's love (*agape* love)? List some thoughts.

9. What popular phrase do you find in 1 John 4:8?

    <u>God   is   love .</u>

    Who likes to quote this phrase, regardless of its context?
    (Circle) your answer.

    Those with the Spirit of truth   Those with the spirit of error

10. Look up the following verses and note what they have to say about who God is.

    Exodus 15:11

    Deuteronomy 10:12

    Joshua 24:14

    Sometimes do I get caught up in worshipping idols?

    Idols - Anything I put before God.

Isaiah 6:3 *his glory*

Gospel of John 4:24

1 John 1:5 (Remember that light is a reference to holiness.)

Revelation 15:3-4 *just + true*

Based on your answers, what does it mean to say that "God is love"?
What does it *not* mean?

*love has many different forms -
correction, judgmental, ~~eor~~*

11. **APPLY:** Why do you think the idea that "God is love" is so popular with
the world? How do our human notions of what love is pollute the way we
think about this phrase, even as believers?

Day Three

NOW LOOK AT 1 JOHN 4:9-18.

12. Why did God send His Son into the world?

Verse 9   live through Him

Verse 10

Verse 14

13. In 1 John 4:12, John says, "No one has ever seen God." Why is this? Look up the following verses to confirm your answer.

Exodus 33:18-20

Gospel of John 4:24

14. How does the second half of 1 John 4:12 explain how people can "see" an invisible God? Look at Gospel of John 13:35 and 17:20-21 to confirm your answer.

15. In 1 John 4:12-18, mark each occurrence of the word *perfected/perfect* with a brown circle.

16. Look up *perfect* (noun) in the dictionary or thesaurus. Circle the synonyms for how you think the word *perfect* is being used in this context.

PERFECT			
Flawless	Expert	Proficient	Pure
Complete	Certain	Mature	Faultless

17. Look up Hebrews 12:2. Who brings about perfection in us?

_____

18. **APPLY:** Think about an area of your life where you have striven for perfection (or near-perfection). Describe that process. How successful were you?

By contrast, does the perfecting of God's love in us (its maturing, purifying, completing work) require effort on our part? Explain your answer.

Day Four

NOW LOOK AGAIN AT 1 JOHN 4:17-18.

19. If agape love is perfected (made complete) in us, what will be the result?

1 John 4:17   boldness

1 John 4:18   perfect love casteth out fear

20. Why does perfect, mature, complete love cast out fears about the "day of judgment" and punishment from God (v. 17)?

21. Read Luke 12:1-12,22-34. Note the sources of fears that occur in these passages. To help you read for detail, number them in the order that Jesus addresses them.

_____ Fears about others

_____ Fears about circumstances

_____ Fears about God

22. **APPLY:** What are some of your fears . . .

. . . about God?

never measure up

. . . about others?

dont fit

belonging -
invest -

. . . about circumstances?

Constant failure

How does the perfect love of Christ address each one of these fears? Note your thoughts next to each fear you listed.

Day Five

READ 1 JOHN 4:19-21.

23. What kind of person is described in these verses?

love vs. fear
love

24. What should be our motive for loving others (v. 19)? What lesser motives do we tend to have for loving others?

25. **APPLY:** Most of us know the tension of simultaneously loving God but very much wanting to withhold our love from a person in our lives who is difficult to love. What is John's message to us regarding these hard relationships? How can you apply this message to a hard relationship in your life?

Wrap-up

What aspect of God's character has this week's passage of 1 John shown you more clearly?

Fill in the following statement:

Knowing that God is _____ shows me that I am _____.

What one step can you take this week to better live in light of this truth?

Lori - where to plug in
path to pursue Anna
safe work/travels for son.

Good Samaritan
I am the man in the ditch.
Jesus is the Good Samaritan -
always coming back! ♡

1. **OBSERVE:** (question 10, p. 92) Based on your answers to the first part of question 10, what does it mean to say that "God is love"? What does it *not* mean?

   APPLY: (question 11, p. 92) Why do you think the idea that "God is love" is so popular with the world? How do our human notions of what love is pollute the way we think about this phrase, even as believers?

2. **OBSERVE:** (question 14, p. 93) How does the second half of 1 John 4:12 explain how people can "see" an invisible God? Look at Gospel of John 13:35 and 17:20-21 to confirm your answer.

   APPLY: (question 18, p. 94) Think about an area of your life where you have striven for perfection (or near-perfection). Describe that process. How successful were you?

   By contrast, does the perfecting of God's love in us (its maturing, purifying, completing work) require effort on our part? Explain your answer.

3. **OBSERVE:** (question 20, p. 95) Why does perfect, mature, complete love cast out fears about the "day of judgment" and punishment from God (v. 17)?

   APPLY: (question 22, p. 96) What are some of your fears about God? About others? About circumstances?

   How does the perfect love of Christ address each one of these fears? Note your thoughts next to each fear you listed.

4. OBSERVE: (question 24, p. 97) What should be our motive for loving others (v. 19)? What lesser motives do we tend to have for loving others?

APPLY: (question 25, p. 97) Most of us know the tension of simultaneously loving God but very much wanting to withhold our love from a person in our lives who is difficult to love. What is John's message to us regarding these hard relationships? How can you apply this message to a hard relationship in your life?

5. WRAP-UP: (p. 98) What aspect of God's character has this week's passage of 1 John shown you more clearly?

Fill in the following statement:

Knowing that God is _____ *shows me that I am* _____ .

What one step can you take this week to better live in light of this truth?

WEEK SIX | VIEWER GUIDE NOTES

To access the video teaching sessions, use the instructions in the back of your workbook.

Week Seven

OVERCOMING THE WORLD

Day One

Remember to take time this week to read through 1, 2, and 3 John from beginning to end. Spend some time committing to memory the passage you chose last week.

READ THIS WEEK'S SECTION OF TEXT: 1 JOHN 5:1-12.

Last week we considered what it means to make the statement "God is love." We learned that God's love perfected in us removes our fears of God's judgment against us.

1. Summarize this section of the text in two to three sentences.

2. Continue your annotating as in previous weeks. Read through the text several times, marking two key words each time you read. Focus on how the words shape the meaning of 1 John.
    ☐ Mark the word *life/live* in green.
    ☐ Circle each occurrence of the phrase *born of God/him* in green.
    ☐ Mark the word *know/known* in blue. Above it, note its meaning in the context of the sentence.
    ☐ Mark every occurrence of the word *children* by circling it in red.
    ☐ Mark every occurrence of the word *brother* by circling it in orange.
    ☐ Mark each occurrence of the word *love* with a red heart.
    ☐ Mark every occurrence of the word *world* with a blue circle.
    ☐ Mark every occurrence of the words *true/truth/confess* in orange. Mark every occurrence of the words *lie/liar/deny/deceive/does not confess/error* in purple.
    ☐ Mark every occurrence of the word *commandment(s)* with a gray underline. You may want to draw a small icon of the Ten Commandments above it.

3. What does this passage teach us about God? Note your observations.

LOOK AT 1 JOHN 5:1-2.

4. What thought from the previous section does verse 1 continue?

5. In verse 2, John uses his much repeated phrase "By this we know . . ." for an eighth and final time. Read the verse and note "by what" we know that we love our fellow brothers in Christ.

6. Compare verse 2 in the NLT and NIV. Rewrite it in your own words.

7. Look back through the first four chapters of 1 John and note below the seven other passages where John has already introduced the thought of "by this we know . . ." You can annotate them in your copy of the text if you like. Choose a colored pencil and annotation symbol that make your heart happy.

8. **APPLY:** How does obeying God's commandments demonstrate love toward others? Choose a clear commandment from the Bible and describe how obeying it is a loving act.

Day Two

NOW READ 1 JOHN 5:3.

9. In verse 3, John claims that God's "commandments are not burdensome."
    Why do you think John makes this point?

10. Look up the word *burdensome* in a dictionary or thesaurus. (It may help to
    look up the root word *burden*.) Write a definition that best fits the way it
    is used in the passage.

BURDENSOME

11. Now rewrite verse 3 in your own words, using your definition for
    burdensome.

12. Now look up the following verses and note what they have to say
    about burdens.

    Psalm 38:4

    Matthew 11:28-30 (Read it in the ESV and CSB.)

According to these verses:
What is burdensome to those who love God?

What is not burdensome to those who love God?

13. **APPLY:** Which of God's commands does the world find burdensome? Give specific examples. What does this reveal about their understanding of the loving fatherhood of God?

Which of God's commands do you tend to find burdensome? Be specific. What does this reveal about your understanding of the loving fatherhood of God?

Day Three

NOW READ 1 JOHN 5:4-5.

14. What do 1 John 5:4-5 tell us keeping God's commandments will enable us to do?

_____ the _____

15. Look up the word *overcome* in a dictionary or thesaurus. Based on what you find, write a definition that best fits the way the word is used in the passage.

OVERCOME

16. Based on your definition above and our previous discussions of the world as *kosmos* (Week Three, Day Five), the seductive world system that opposes Christ, what do you think it means to "overcome the world"?

17. Look back through the first four chapters of 1 John, and note the passage(s) where John has already introduced the idea of overcoming the world.

18. Why are Christians described as those who overcome the world? Look up the Gospel of John 16:33 to help with your answer.

19. **APPLY:** Think of the Christians you know. Would you describe them as people who overcome (prevail over, gain victory over) the world (the world's system of belief)? Why or why not?

How has your own life shown evidence of overcoming the world? Where do you have the most difficulty prevailing?

Day Four

NOW READ 1 JOHN 5:6-12.

20. With a pink highlighter, mark each occurrence of the word *testify/testifies* or *testimony*. Look up the words *testify* and *testimony* in a dictionary or thesaurus. Based on what you find, write definitions that best fit the way the words are used in the passage.

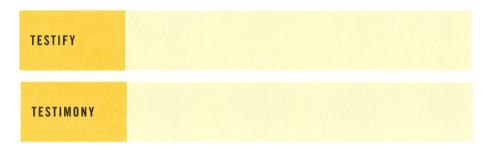

| TESTIFY | |
| TESTIMONY | |

Make a list of everything or everyone in 1 John 5:6-12 that testifies.

Verse	Who/What Testifies

To what (or whom) do all of these things testify?

21. **APPLY:** Think of a powerful testimony of eternal life in Christ that you have heard from another believer. How did it influence your faith?

Day Five

NOW CONSIDER THE IMPLICATIONS OF THE THINGS THAT TESTIFY IN 1 JOHN 5:6-12.

22. We will spend time in the teaching discussing why John says that Jesus came by *water* and by *blood*. For now, take your best shot at explaining what you think he means. What do you think water and blood refer to?

    WATER:

    BLOOD:

23. On what do the Spirit, the water, and the blood agree (vv. 8,11)?

24. Look back to 1 John 1:2 and 4:14, and highlight in pink where John earlier introduced the theme of testifying to the eternal life in Christ.

25. What do you think John means by "the testimony of God is greater" than the testimony of men (v. 9)? Where is the testimony of God to the truth of eternal life in Christ found? How is it proclaimed?

26. **APPLY:** How does your personal testimony of eternal life in Christ and faith in Him add to the weight of evidence that Jesus is the Christ? In other words, how does your story of redemption bear witness to the truth of the gospel?

Wrap-up

What aspect of God's character has this week's passage of 1 John shown you more clearly?

Fill in the following statement:

Knowing that God is _____ *shows me that I am* _____ .

What one step can you take this week to better live in light of this truth?

WEEK SEVEN | GROUP DISCUSSION

1. OBSERVE: (question 4, p. 107) What thought from the previous section does verse 1 continue?

APPLY: (question 7, p. 108) How does obeying God's commandments demonstrate love toward others? Choose a clear commandment from the Bible and describe how obeying it is a loving act.

2. OBSERVE: (question 9, p. 109) In verse 3, John claims that God's "commandments are not burdensome." Why do you think John makes this point?

APPLY: (question 13, p. 110) Which of God's commands does the world find burdensome? Give specific examples. What does this reveal about their understanding of the loving fatherhood of God?

Which of God's commands do you tend to find burdensome? Be specific. What does this reveal about your understanding of the loving fatherhood of God?

3. OBSERVE: (question 18, p. 112) Why are Christians described as those who overcome the world? Look up the Gospel of John 16:33 to help with your answer.

APPLY: (question 19, p. 112) Think of the Christians you know. Would you describe them as people who overcome (prevail over, gain victory over) the world (the world's system of belief)? Why or why not?

How has your own life shown evidence of overcoming the world? Where do you have the most difficulty prevailing?

4. OBSERVE: (question 25, p. 114) What do you think John means by "the testimony of God is greater" than the testimony of men (v. 9)? Where is the testimony of God to the truth of eternal life in Christ found? How is it proclaimed?

APPLY: (question 26, p. 115) How does your personal testimony of eternal life in Christ and faith in Him add to the weight of evidence that Jesus is the Christ? In other words, how does your story of redemption bear witness to the truth of the gospel?

5. WRAP-UP: (p. 116) What aspect of God's character has this week's passage of 1 John shown you more clearly?

Fill in the following statement:

Knowing that God is _____ *shows me that I am* _____.

What one step can you take this week to better live in light of this truth?

WEEK SEVEN | VIEWER GUIDE NOTES

To access the video teaching sessions, use the instructions in the back of your workbook.

1 JOHN 5:13-21

Week Eight

THAT YOU MAY KNOW

Day One

Remember to take time this week to read through 1, 2, and, 3 John from beginning to end. Spend some time committing to memory the passage you chose.

READ THIS WEEK'S SECTION OF TEXT: 1 JOHN 5:13-21.

Last week we considered what it means that the Spirit and the water and the blood testify to the truth of Jesus Christ. We learned that the testimony of God is greater than the testimony of man.

1. Summarize this section of the text in two to three sentences.

2. Continue your annotating as in previous weeks. Read through the text several times, marking two key words each time you read. Focus on how the words shape the meaning of 1 John.

    ☐ Mark the word *life/live* in green.

    ☐ Circle each occurrence of the phrase *born of God/him* in green.

    ☐ Mark the word *know/known* in blue. Above it, note its meaning in the context of the sentence.

    ☐ Mark every occurrence of the word *children* by circling it in red.

    ☐ Mark every occurrence of the word *brother* by circling it in orange.

    ☐ Mark every occurrence of the word *world* with a blue circle.

    ☐ Mark the phrase *evil one* with a red devil head.

3. What does this passage teach us about God? Note your observations.

4. You may have noted that this final section of John's letter is concerned with knowing certain truths. We will examine this idea as we move through our lesson. How many times does the word *know* appear in these nine final verses? _____

Day Two

LOOK AT 1 JOHN 5:13.

5. In Week Two of your homework, we noted two reasons John gave for writing his letter. In verse 13, he gives a third and final reason. Note all three reasons.

Verse	Reason John Writes
1:4	
2:1	
5:13	

6. What is the shared desire all three of John's reasons express?

7. During the course of his letter, what evidence has John given his readers that they might "know that [they] have eternal life" (v. 13)?

8. We have noted similarities between the Gospel of John and the epistles (letters) of John throughout our study. You may remember from the beginning of our study that both the Gospel of John and 1 John begin with very similar wording and ideas. (Compare John 1:1-5 with 1 John 1:1-5.) They also end with similar ideas. Compare the Gospel of John 20:30-31 to 1 John 5:13. What similar message do these passages contain?

9. **APPLY:** Why would John's original audience have needed assurance that they had eternal life?

Why do *we* need this assurance? How does such an assurance impact the way we think about and live our lives in the present?

Day Three

LOOK AT 1 JOHN 5:14-15.

10. In verse 14, John mentions the idea of our confidence before God a fourth and final time. Look back at the first three mentions and note what aspect of our confidence they highlight.

2:28

3:20-21

4:17

Specifically, what kind of confidence does 5:14 say we should have? How does this kind of confidence relate to John's earlier mentions of the idea?

11. What does John want us to "know" in verse 15?

12. In verses 14-15, what requests does John assure us will be granted by our Father?

13. How can a believer know whether her requests are being made in accordance with the will of the Father? Look up the Gospel of John 15:7 to help with your answer.

14. Give some examples of things we can always ask for that are in accordance with God's will.

15. **APPLY:** When you make requests of God, are they typically requests like those you listed above? Should they be? Are other types of requests also valid? Explain your answer.

Day Four

NOW LOOK AT 1 JOHN 5:16-17.

16. What does John want us to "know" in these verses?

17. According to 1 John 5:16-17, what is our responsibility to our fellow believers with whom we have fellowship?

18. Verses 16-17 have been interpreted various ways. We will discuss these verses during the teaching time, but try to form your own interpretation before then. What do you think John means when he says there is sin which leads to death? Compare this passage to 1 John 3:4-10 to help you with your answer.

19. **APPLY:** When you see a fellow believer sinning, is your first action to ask God to deliver that person from his or her sin? What other actions do we sometimes take before we remember to pray for our brother or sister? Why is this so?

Day Five

NOW LOOK AT 1 JOHN 5:18-20.

20. In verses 18-20, John concludes by reiterating three things we know. What are they?

Verse 18

Verse 19

Verse 20

21. There are some confusing "*he*s" and "*him*s" in verse 18. Read the verse carefully in the ESV and the NIV, identifying who you think each "him" refers to. Then rewrite the verse in your own words in the space below. Substitute proper nouns in place of pronouns.

22. How do we reconcile John's statement that "the evil one does not touch him" who "was born of God" (v. 18) with the reality that believers do continue to sin?

23. **APPLY:** Describe a time when you felt the protection of the Lord in the midst of temptation, keeping you from sin.

Do we always see God's protection from sin at the time it is being given? Think of a time you realized in hindsight that the Lord had protected you from sin. Describe it below.

How might reflecting on the past faithfulness of God, seen in hindsight, change the way we make requests for His help in a current area of temptation?

24. Why do you think John concludes his letter with the statement, "Little children, keep yourselves from idols" (v. 21)? How does this thought connect to the rest of the letter?

25. **APPLY:** One of the definitions of the word *idol* found in the dictionary or thesaurus is "a false conception." What false conceptions of God has 1 John revealed in your heart? If you have difficulty answering this question, think back to the things you fear. Remembering that our fears are based in some false conception of God's character, what do your fears reveal about wrong ideas of God you may be holding onto?

Wrap-up

What aspect of God's character has this week's passage of 1 John shown you more clearly?

Fill in the following statement:

Knowing that God is _____ shows me that I am _____.

What one step can you take this week to better live in light of this truth?

WEEK EIGHT | GROUP DISCUSSION

1. OBSERVE: (question 7, p. 126) During the course of his letter, what evidence has John given his readers that they might "know that [they] have eternal life" (v. 13)?

APPLY: (question 9, p. 127) Why would John's original audience have needed assurance that they had eternal life?

Why do *we* need this assurance? How does such an assurance impact the way we think about and live our lives in the present?

2. OBSERVE: (question 14, p. 129) Give some examples of things we can always ask for that are in accordance with God's will.

APPLY: (question 15, p. 129) When you make requests of God, are they typically requests like those you listed? Should they be? Are other types of requests also valid? Explain your answer.

3. OBSERVE: (question 17, p. 130) According to 1 John 5:16-17, what is our responsibility to our fellow believers with whom we have fellowship?

APPLY: (question 19, p. 130) When you see a fellow believer sinning, is your first action to ask God to deliver that person from his or her sin? What other actions do we sometimes take before we remember to pray for our brother or sister? Why is this so?

4. OBSERVE: (question 20, p. 131) In verses 18-20, John concludes by reiterating three things we know. What are they?

APPLY: (question 23, p. 132) Describe a time when you felt the protection of the Lord in the midst of temptation, keeping you from sin.

Do we always see God's protection from sin at the time it is being given? Think of a time you realized in hindsight that the Lord had protected you from sin. Describe it.

How might reflecting on the past faithfulness of God, seen in hindsight, change the way we make requests for His help in a current area of temptation?

5. **WRAP-UP:** (p. 133) What aspect of God's character has this week's passage of 1 John shown you more clearly?

Fill in the following statement:

Knowing that God is _____ *shows me that I am* _____.

What one step can you take this week to better live in light of this truth?

WEEK EIGHT | VIEWER GUIDE NOTES

To access the video teaching sessions, use the instructions in the back of your workbook.

2 JOHN

Week
Nine

WALK IN TRUTH AND LOVE

Day One

Remember to take time this week to read through 1, 2, and 3 John from beginning to end. Spend some time committing to memory the passage you chose. Try reciting it aloud to someone.

LOOK AT THIS WEEK'S TEXT: 2 JOHN 1-13.

Last week we concluded our study of 1 John with assurances of what we know to be true and an admonition to avoid idolatry. This week we will study 2 John in its entirety. We will look for how it is similar to 1 John in language and themes, and we will look for new themes it introduces.

1. Summarize 2 John in two to three sentences.

Asia minor - written to church "women".
written to
1) encourage to continue in truth
2) exhort to seperate falsehood
3) joy + blessing from lord
4) relationship w/ God for those walking w/ Lord.

2. Continue your annotating as in previous weeks, marking in 2 John each of the key words we have identified in 1 John. Read through the text several times, marking two key words each time you read. Focus on how the words shape the meaning of 2 John.

☐ Mark the phrase "from the beginning" (v. 1) in pink. Draw a tiny clock face above it.

☐ Mark the word *know/known* in blue. Above it, note its meaning in the context of the sentence.

☐ Mark every occurrence of the word *children* by circling it in red.

☐ Mark each occurrence of the word *love* with a red heart.

☐ Mark every occurrence of the word *world* with a blue circle.

☐ Mark every occurrence of the words *true/truth/confess* in orange. Mark every occurrence of the words *lie/liar/deny/deceive/does not confess/error* in purple.

☐ Mark every occurrence of the word *commandment(s)* with a gray underline. You may also want to draw a small icon of the Ten Commandments above it.

☐ Highlight the word *abide* in yellow.

☐ Mark the word *antichrist* with a red devil head.

3. Marking the same repeated words and phrases from 1 John shows how much 2 John has in common with it. What differences do you find? Are any new ideas introduced? Any new directions of thought explored? Note them and the verses where you found them.

4. What does 2 John teach us about God? Note your observations.

Day Two

LOOK AT 2 JOHN 1-3.

5. The letter of 2 John may be written to a literal woman and her children, or it may be written to a church. Based on how you read the letter, which do you think is more likely? Why? Give verses to support your answer.

6. What does John mean by the term *elect*? Read verse 1 in the NIV to help with your answer.

7. How does verse 3 enrich your understanding of what a gift it is to be chosen by God? What unlooked for gain is ours?

   Grace - security, undeserved
   mercy -
   peace - blessing of Grace + mercy
   truth
   love

8. **APPLY:** How have you been the recipient of each of the three gifts John mentions at the beginning of verse 3? How have you witnessed them in your life? How have you witnessed them in the past month?

   watch videos : truth + Love
   ↳ legalist   ↳ yes Mom

Day Three

NOW LOOK AT 2 JOHN 1-6.

9. In the first four verses, how many times does John use the word *truth*?
    Note everything you learn about the truth in verses 1-4.

10. Based on what you noted above about *truth*, what does John mean by
    "whom I love in truth" in verse 1? Look up the Gospel of John 14:6 and
    then check the best answer.

    my relationship w/ my mom - truth + not love

    _____ whom I really, truly love

    _____ whose truthfulness I love

    _____ whom I love in Christ, who is Truth

11. How is "walking in the truth" (2 John 4) different than knowing or
    believing the truth?

12. **APPLY:** The Bible teaches truth about pride, worry, lust, laziness,
    anger, gossip, and much more. What biblical truth do you know and
    believe but struggle to walk in? How can you move from intellectual
    assent to obedience?

13. In the first six verses, how many times does John use the word *love*? Note everything you learn about love in 2 John 1-6.

14. John speaks of the commandment that we "have heard from the beginning" (v. 6). What is it?

15. Note in verse 6 how John defines love for one another. Fill in the blanks.

    And this is love, that we _____ according to _____

    _____.

    Does this definition surprise you? What other ways do we define love for one another? How is John's definition of brotherly love accurate and practical?

16. What point in time does John refer to when he says "from the beginning"?
    Is it the same "from the beginning" mentioned in 1 John 1:1 or in
    1 John 2:24? Explain your answer.

17. **APPLY:** Why do we need to understand both truth and love? What can
    happen if we walk in one without the other? Give an example.

    What relationship in your life would improve if you walked in greater
    truth toward that person?

    my mom. How to improve it?

    What relationship in your life would improve if you walked in greater love
    toward that person?

Day Four

LOOK AT 2 JOHN 7-8.

18. Look at verse 7. Compare it to 1 John 2:22 and 1 John 4:2-3. What is the consistent definition of an antichrist or false teacher?

19. Why is denying that Jesus came in the flesh such a terrible deception to teach?

    John 3:16 For God so loved the world...

    Philippians 2:6-8

20. Why is it important that Jesus Christ was human? Why is it important that Jesus Christ was also God? What danger is there in believing He was one or the other, but not both?

21. In verse 8, who is the "you" that John warns might lose what has been worked for? Consider the context, then check the answer you think is correct.

    _____ unbelievers

    _____ believers

    _____ false teachers

22. Look at verse 8. When John speaks of not losing "what we have worked for," how can we know he is not speaking of losing our salvation? Look up the following passages to help with your answer.

Gospel of John 6:39

Gospel of John 10:27-30

Philippians 1:6

Titus 3:5

23. Look up the word *reward* in a dictionary or thesaurus. Write a definition for it that best fits with the way it is used in verse 8.

REWARD (noun)

How does your definition further clarify that John is not speaking of losing our salvation? Compare Ephesians 2:8-9 to confirm your answer.

24. What "reward" is John speaking of? Look up 1 Corinthians 3:11-13 to help with your answer.

work is tried by fire
malachi 3:2-3

25. **APPLY:** How should the believer feel about the fact that salvation cannot be earned or lost, but that our righteous deeds will be rewarded? How do these two ideas give you both assurance and warning?

Perspective
∅ selfishness
what are righteous deeds?

Day Five

LOOK AT 2 JOHN 9-13.

26. What do you think it means to "[go] on ahead" versus to "abide in the teaching of Christ" (v. 9)? Rewrite verse 9 in your own words.

27. Read verses 10-11 in the ESV and the NIV. How does John say believers are to act toward deceivers who seek out our hospitality?

28. Is John saying that we should not show hospitality to unbelievers or to those whose beliefs do not align perfectly with our own? Explain your answer.

29. Why do you think John wanted to meet face to face with the recipients of his letter (vv. 12-13)?

30. What sorts of conversations are better handled face to face?

31. **APPLY:** Think about a time when you tried to address something via letter, email, or text that would have been better handled face to face. What happened? How would having a face-to-face conversation have better allowed you to maintain Christlikeness?

The abundant life
joy, gratitude
brings more fulness
of life.

Wrap-up

What aspect of God's character has 2 John shown you more clearly?

Walking in truth + love

Matt 7:6

Fill in the following statement:

Knowing that God is _____ shows me that I am _____.

What one step can you take this week to better live in light of this truth?

WEEK NINE | GROUP DISCUSSION

1. OBSERVE: (question 7, p. 142) How does verse 3 enrich your understanding of what a gift it is to be chosen by God? What unlooked for gain is ours?

APPLY: (question 8, p. 142) How have you been the recipient of each of the three gifts John mentions at the beginning of verse 3? How have you witnessed them in your life? How have you witnessed them in the past month?

2. OBSERVE: (question 11, p. 143) How is "walking in the truth" (2 John 4) different than knowing or believing the truth?

APPLY: (question 12, p. 143) The Bible teaches truth about pride, worry, lust, laziness, anger, gossip, and much more. What biblical truth do you know and believe but struggle to walk in? How can you move from intellectual assent to obedience?

3. OBSERVE: (question 20, p. 146) Why is it important that Jesus Christ was human? Why is it important that Jesus Christ was also God? What danger is there in believing He was one or the other, but not both?

APPLY: (question 25, p. 147) How should the believer feel about the fact that salvation cannot be earned or lost, but that our righteous deeds will be rewarded? How do these two ideas give you both assurance and warning?

4. OBSERVE: (question 29, p. 148) Why do you think John wanted to meet face to face with the recipients of his letter (vv. 12-13)?

APPLY: (question 31, p. 148) Think about a time when you tried to address something via letter, email, or text that would have been better handled face to face. What happened? How would having a face-to-face conversation have better allowed you to maintain Christlikeness?

5. WRAP-UP: (p. 149) What aspect of God's character has 2 John shown you more clearly?

Fill in the following statement:

Knowing that God is _____ *shows me that I am* _____.

What one step can you take this week to better live in light of this truth?

WEEK NINE | VIEWER GUIDE NOTES

To access the video teaching sessions, use the instructions in the back of your workbook.

Week
Ten

IMITATE GOOD

Day One

Remember to take time this week to read through 1, 2, and 3 John from beginning to end. Spend some time committing to memory the passage you chose.

READ THIS WEEK'S TEXT: 3 JOHN 1-15.

Last week we listened in on John's instructions to a group of believers regarding how they could walk in truth and love, particularly with regard to dealing with false teachers. This week we will study 3 John in its entirety. We will look for how it is similar to 1 and 2 John in language and themes, and we will look for new themes it introduces.

1. Summarize 3 John in two to three sentences.

2. Continue your annotating as in previous weeks, marking in 3 John each of the key words we have identified in 1 and 2 John. Read through the text several times, marking two key words each time you read. Focus on how the words shape the meaning of 3 John.

   □ Mark the word *know/known* in blue. Above it, note its meaning in the context of the sentence.

   □ Mark every occurrence of the word *children* by circling it in red.

   □ Mark every occurrence of the word *testify/testimony* with a pink highlighter.

   □ Mark every occurrence of the word *practice(s)/does* with a black underline.

   □ Mark every occurrence of the word *brother* by circling it in orange.

   □ Mark each occurrence of the word *love* with a red heart.

   □ Mark every occurrence of the words *true/truth/confess* in orange. Mark every occurrence of the words *lie/liar/deny/deceive/does not confess/error* in purple (Hint: the idea, but not the exact word *lie* is found in verse 10).

3. Marking the same repeated words and phrases from 1 and 2 John shows how much 3 John has in common with them. What differences do you find? Are any new ideas introduced? Any new directions of thought explored? Note them, and the verses where you found them.

4. What does 3 John teach us about God? Note your observations.

Day Two

LOOK AT 3 JOHN 1-4.

5. How is the salutation of 3 John 1-4 similar to that of 2 John 1-3? How is it different?

SIMILAR	DIFFERENT

6. What adjective does John use to describe Gaius (v. 1)?

_____

How many times does he repeat the term in the letter? _____

Look up 3 John 1 in the CSB. How is the same word translated there?

_____

What does the use of this term establish about the tone of John's letter?

7. Who do you think the brothers who "came and testified to your truth" are (v. 3)? Compare verse 3 in the CSB and NIV. Then rewrite it in your own words.

8. What does John indicate is his greatest joy? State it in your own words.

9. **APPLY:** Think about what brings you joy in a relationship. Would you say you have "no greater joy" than seeing the godly obedience of those you love?

What lesser "good things" compete for your joy and approval in your relationships with others? How does rejoicing in lesser things than godly obedience potentially harm our key relationships?

Day Three

LOOK AT 3 JOHN 5-8.

10. What additional insight do we gain about Gaius and his activities? What sort of person does he appear to be? Note everything you learn about him in verses 5-8.

11. What insight do we gain about the "brothers" and their activities? What sort of people do they appear to be? Note everything you learn about them in verses 5-8.

12. What do you think John means by "for the sake of the name" (v. 7)? Read the verse in the ESV and the RSV. Why does John include this detail?

13. Who do you think John means by "the Gentiles" (v. 7)? Read the verse in the ESV and the RSV. Then check the answer that best fits with the context.

_____ non-Jews

_____ unbelievers

14. Why does John mention that the brothers accept "nothing from the Gentiles"? What point is he making?

15. What does John say we become when we offer support and hospitality to other believers doing kingdom work (v. 8)?

16. What kind of support do you think John has in mind for us to offer in verse 8? To help with your answer, look up Philippians 4:14-20 and read how Paul commends those who supported his ministry efforts.

    What was the nature of their support?

    What assurance does Paul give them in light of their faithful giving (v. 19)?

17. **APPLY:** How do you show hospitality and generosity to believers doing kingdom work? Why is it important for Christians to demonstrate hospitality?

    What causes us to hesitate to extend hospitality or generosity? Why are these hesitations unjustified?

Day Four

LOOK AT 3 JOHN 9-10.

18. What problem does John turn his attention to in verses 9-10?

19. What insight do we gain about Diotrephes and his activities? What sort of person does he appear to be? Note everything you learn about him.

20. How many of the Ten Commandments does Diotrephes break? Skim through Exodus 20:1-17 and note them.

21. How does who Diotrephes loves contrast with John's earlier discussions about love in 1 and 2 John? Note any verses that come to mind.

22. **APPLY:** How is a person like Diotrephes potentially harmful to any group or organization, sacred or secular? Why are people like him so damaging to the work of the church, in particular?

Have you ever been in a church with someone (or a group of someones) who acted like Diotrephes? If so, describe what happened. What did you learn from the experience?

Day Five

LOOK AT 3 JOHN 11-15.

23. How does verse 11 flow logically from the previous sections?

24. As he has done elsewhere, in verse 11 John introduces a pair of contrasting terms. What are they?

_____ and _____

25. Which of the people mentioned in 3 John "imitate good"? Which "imitate evil"? Write their names above, underneath the term they imitate.

26. What insight do we gain about Demetrius and his activities? What sort of person does he appear to be? Note what you learn about him.

27. **APPLY:** Who do you know that might be an evil influence you are tempted to imitate? What sinful behaviors do they tempt you to mimic?

Who has the Lord placed in your life as a positive influence to imitate? What Christlike quality they demonstrate would you most like to imitate?

28. Now look at verses 13-15. Compare them to 2 John 12-13. How are these closing comments similar? How are they different?

29. What does 3 John 13-15 reveal about John's character? How do his closing comments model virtues that are Christlike?

30. **APPLY:** We can only greet someone by name if we have taken time to remember his or her name in the first place. How do you feel when someone takes care to learn and remember your name?

Whose name do you have trouble calling to mind when you see him or her? Commit to pray for that person by name this week.

Wrap-up

What aspect of God's character has 3 John shown you more clearly?

Fill in the following statement:

Knowing that God is _____ *shows me that I am* _____.

What one step can you take this week to better live in light of this truth?

WEEK TEN | GROUP DISCUSSION

1. OBSERVE: (question 8, p. 159) What does John indicate is his greatest joy? State it in your own words.

APPLY: (question 9, p. 159) Think about what brings you joy in a relationship. Would you say you have "no greater joy" than seeing the godly obedience of those you love?

What lesser "good things" compete for your joy and approval in your relationships with others? How does rejoicing in lesser things than godly obedience potentially harm our key relationships?

2. OBSERVE: (question 16, p. 161) What kind of support do you think John has in mind for us to offer in verse 8? To help with your answer, look up Philippians 4:14-20 and read how Paul commends those who supported his ministry efforts. What was the nature of their support? What assurance does Paul give them in light of their faithful giving (v. 19)?

APPLY: (question 17, p. 161) How do you show hospitality and generosity to believers doing kingdom work? Why is it important for Christians to demonstrate hospitality?

What causes us to hesitate to extend hospitality or generosity? Why are these hesitations unjustified?

3. OBSERVE: (question 20, p. 162) How many of the Ten Commandments does Diotrephes break? Skim through Exodus 20:1-17 and note them.

APPLY: (question 22, p. 162) How is a person like Diotrephes potentially harmful to any group or organization, sacred or secular? Why are people like him so damaging to the work of the church, in particular?

Have you ever been in a church with someone (or a group of someones) who acted like Diotrephes? If so, describe what happened. What did you learn from the experience?

4. **OBSERVE:** (question 29, p. 164) What does 3 John 13-15 reveal about John's character? How do his closing comments model virtues that are Christlike?

APPLY: (question 30, p. 164) We can only greet someone by name if we have taken time to remember his or her name in the first place. How do you feel when someone takes care to learn and remember your name?

Whose name do you have trouble calling to mind when you see him or her? Commit to pray for that person by name this week.

5. **WRAP-UP:** (p. 165) What aspect of God's character has 3 John shown you more clearly?

Fill in the following statement:

Knowing that God is _____ shows me
that I am _____.

What one step can you take this week to better live in light of this truth?

WEEK TEN | VIEWER GUIDE NOTES

To access the video teaching sessions, use the instructions in the back of your workbook.

Wrap-up

For ten weeks, you have had the rich blessing of learning at the feet of John, the disciple whom Jesus loved. Take some time to reflect on what you will take away from this study. Can you guess where a good place to start might be? That's right—by reading through 1, 2, and 3 John one last time. As you take your "victory lap," pay special attention to what stands out most in your mind from your weeks in these three little letters tucked at the end of the New Testament.

READ STRAIGHT THROUGH 1, 2, AND 3 JOHN.

As you read, think back on what you've learned throughout your study. Answer the following questions.

1. What attribute of God has emerged most clearly as you have studied this letter?

    How does knowing this truth about Him change the way you see yourself?

    How should knowing this truth change the way you live?

2. How has the Holy Spirit used 1, 2, and 3 John to convict you of sin? What thoughts, words, or actions has He shown you that need to be redeemed? What do you need to stop doing?

3. How has the Holy Spirit used 1, 2, and 3 John to train you in righteousness? What disciplines has He given you a desire to pursue? What do you need to start doing?

4. How has the Holy Spirit used 1, 2, and 3 John to encourage you? What cause to celebrate have John's letters imprinted on your heart?

5. What verse or passage from John's letters stands out most in your mind after ten weeks of study? Why?

CLOSE IN PRAYER. Thank God for giving us the example of John, beloved by Jesus, who abided in Him to the end of his days. Thank God for giving us Christ, fully God and fully man, before whom we can stand with confidence, who has shown to us a selfless and purposeful agape love. Ask Him to keep you ever mindful of "that which you have heard from the beginning." Thank Him that you are His little child.

1, 2, 3 JOHN

1 JOHN 1

The Word of Life

[1] That which was from the beginning, which we have heard, which we have seen with our eyes, which we looked upon and have touched with our hands, concerning the word of life— [2] the life was made manifest, and we have seen it, and testify to it and proclaim to you the eternal life, which was with the Father and was made manifest to us—

[3] that which we have seen and heard we proclaim also to you, so that you too may have fellowship with us; and indeed our fellowship is with the Father and with his Son Jesus Christ. [4] And we are writing these things so that our joy may be complete.

Walking in the Light

[5] This is the message we have heard from him and proclaim to you, that God is light, and in him is no darkness at all. [6] If we say we have fellowship with him while we walk in darkness, we lie and do not practice the truth. [7] But if we walk in the light, as he is in the light, we have fellowship with one another, and the blood of Jesus his Son cleanses us from all sin. [8] If we say we have no sin, we deceive ourselves, and the truth is not in us. [9] If we confess our sins, he is faithful and just to forgive us our sins and to cleanse us from all unrighteousness. [10] If we say we have not sinned, we make him a liar, and his word is not in us.

Christt Our Advocate

[1] My little children, I am writing these things to you so that you may not sin. But if anyone does sin, we have an advocate with the Father, Jesus Christ the righteous. [2] He is the propitiation for our sins, and not for ours only but also for the sins of the whole world. [3] And by this we know that we have come to know him, if we keep his commandments. [4] Whoever says "I know him" but does not keep his commandments is a liar, and the truth is not in him, [5] but whoever keeps his word, in him truly the love of God is perfected. By this we may know that we are in him: [6] whoever says he abides in him ought to walk in the same way in which he walked.

The New Commandment

[7] Beloved, I am writing you no new commandment, but an old commandment that you had from the beginning. The old commandment is the word that you have heard. [8] At the same time, it is a new commandment that I am writing to you, which is true in him and in you, because the darkness is passing away and the true light is already shining. [9] Whoever says he is in the light and hates his brother is still in darkness. [10] Whoever loves his brother abides in the light, and in him there is no cause for stumbling. [11] But whoever hates his brother is in the darkness and walks in the darkness, and does not know where he is going, because the darkness has blinded his eyes.

[12] I am writing to you, little children,

    because your sins are forgiven for his name's sake.

[13] I am writing to you, fathers,

    because you know him who is from the beginning.

I am writing to you, young men,

    because you have overcome the evil one.

I write to you, children,

because you know the Father.

[14] I write to you, fathers,

because you know him who is from the beginning.

I write to you, young men,

because you are strong,

and the word of God abides in you,

and you have overcome the evil one.

Do Not Love the World

[15] Do not love the world or the things in the world. If anyone loves the world, the love of the Father is not in him. [16] For all that is in the world—the desires of the flesh and the desires of the eyes and pride of life—is not from the Father but is from the world. [17] And the world is passing away along with its desires, but whoever does the will of God abides forever.

Warning Concerning Antichrists

[18] Children, it is the last hour, and as you have heard that antichrist is coming, so now many antichrists have come. Therefore we know that it is the last hour. [19] They went out from us, but they were not of us; for if they had been of us, they would have continued with us. But they went out, that it might become plain that they all are not of us. [20] But you have been anointed by the Holy One, and you all have knowledge. [21] I write to you, not because you do not know the truth, but because you know it, and because no lie is of the truth. [22] Who is the liar but he who denies that Jesus is the Christ? This is the antichrist, he who denies the Father and the Son. [23] No one who denies the Son has the Father. Whoever confesses the Son has the Father also. [24] Let what you heard from the beginning abide in you. If what you heard from the beginning abides in you, then you too will abide in the Son and in the Father. [25] And this is the promise that he made to us—eternal life.

[26] I write these things to you about those who are trying to deceive you. [27] But the anointing that you received from him abides in you, and you have no need that anyone

should teach you. But as his anointing teaches you about everything, and is true, and is no lie—just as it has taught you, abide in him.

Children of God

[28] And now, little children, abide in him, so that when he appears we may have confidence and not shrink from him in shame at his coming. [29] If you know that he is righteous, you may be sure that everyone who practices righteousness has been born of him.

1 JOHN 3

[1] See what kind of love the Father has given to us, that we should be called children of God; and so we are. The reason why the world does not know us is that it did not know him. [2] Beloved, we are God's children now, and what we will be has not yet appeared; but we know that when he appears we shall be like him, because we shall see him as he is. [3] And everyone who thus hopes in him purifies himself as he is pure.

[4] Everyone who makes a practice of sinning also practices lawlessness; sin is lawlessness. [5] You know that he appeared in order to take away sins, and in him there is no sin. [6] No one who abides in him keeps on sinning; no one who keeps on sinning has either seen him or known him. [7] Little children, let no one deceive you. Whoever practices righteousness is righteous, as he is righteous. [8] Whoever makes a practice of sinning is of the devil, for the devil has been sinning from the beginning. The reason the Son of God appeared was to destroy the works of the devil. [9] No one born of God makes a practice of sinning, for God's seed abides in him; and he cannot keep on sinning, because he has been born of God. [10] By this it is evident who are the children of God, and who are the children of the devil: whoever does not practice righteousness is not of God, nor is the one who does not love his brother.

Love One Another

[11] For this is the message that you have heard from the beginning, that we should love one another. [12] We should not be like Cain, who was of the evil one and murdered his brother. And why did he murder him? Because his own deeds were evil and his brother's righteous. [13] Do not be surprised, brothers, that the world hates you. [14] We know that we have passed out of death into life, because we love the brothers. Whoever does not love abides in death. [15] Everyone who hates his brother is a murderer, and you know that no murderer has eternal life abiding in him.

[16] By this we know love, that he laid down his life for us, and we ought to lay down our lives for the brothers. [17] But if anyone has the world's goods and sees his brother in need, yet closes his heart against him, how does God's love abide in him? [18] Little children, let us not love in word or talk but in deed and in truth.

[19] By this we shall know that we are of the truth and reassure our heart before him; [20] for whenever our heart condemns us, God is greater than our heart, and he knows everything. [21] Beloved, if our heart does not condemn us, we have confidence before God; [22] and whatever we ask we receive from him, because we keep his commandments and do what pleases him. [23] And this is his commandment, that we believe in the name of his Son Jesus Christ and love one another, just as he has commanded us. [24] Whoever keeps his commandments abides in God, and God in him. And by this we know that he abides in us, by the Spirit whom he has given us.

Test the Spirits

[1] Beloved, do not believe every spirit, but test the spirits to see whether they are from God, for many false prophets have gone out into the world. [2] By this you know the Spirit of God: every spirit that confesses that Jesus Christ has come in the flesh is from God, [3] and every spirit that does not confess Jesus is not from God. This is the spirit of the antichrist, which you heard was coming and now is in the world already. [4] Little children, you are from God and have overcome them, for he who is in you is greater than he who is in the world. [5] They are from the world; therefore they speak from the world, and the world listens to them. [6] We are from God. Whoever knows God listens to us; whoever is not from God does not listen to us. By this we know the Spirit of truth and the spirit of error.

God Is Love

[7] Beloved, let us love one another, for love is from God, and whoever loves has been born of God and knows God. [8] Anyone who does not love does not know God, because God is love. [9] In this the love of God was made manifest among us, that God sent his only Son into the world, so that we might live through him. [10] In this is love, not that we have loved God but that he loved us and sent his Son to be the propitiation for our sins. [11] Beloved, if God so loved us, we also ought to love one another. [12] No one has ever seen God; if we love one another, God abides in us and his love is perfected in us.

[13] By this we know that we abide in him and he in us, because he has given us of his Spirit. [14] And we have seen and testify that the Father has sent his Son to be the Savior of the world. [15] Whoever confesses that Jesus is the Son of God, God abides in him, and he in God. [16] So we have come to know and to believe the love that God has for us. God is love, and whoever abides in love abides in God, and God abides in him. [17] By this is love perfected with us, so that we may have confidence for the day of judgment, because as he is so also are we in this world. [18] There is no fear in love, but perfect love casts out

fear. For fear has to do with punishment, and <u>whoever fears has not been perfected in</u> <u>love.</u> [19] We love because he first loved us. [20] If anyone says, "I love God," and hates his brother, he is a liar; for he who does not love his brother whom he has seen cannot love God whom he has not seen. [21] And this commandment we have from him: whoever loves God must also love his brother.

1 JOHN 5

Overcoming the World

[1] Everyone who believes that Jesus is the Christ has been born of God, and everyone who loves the Father loves whoever has been born of him. [2] By this we know that we love the children of God, when we love God and obey his commandments. [3] For this is the love of God, that we keep his commandments. And his commandments are not burdensome. [4] For everyone who has been born of God overcomes the world. And this is the victory that has overcome the world—our faith. [5] Who is it that overcomes the world except the one who believes that Jesus is the Son of God?

Testimony Concerning the Son of God

[6] This is he who came by water and blood—Jesus Christ; not by the water only but by the water and the blood. And the Spirit is the one who testifies, because the Spirit is the truth. [7] For there are three that testify: [8] the Spirit and the water and the blood; and these three agree. [9] If we receive the testimony of men, the testimony of God is greater, for this is the testimony of God that he has borne concerning his Son. [10] Whoever believes in the Son of God has the testimony in himself. Whoever does not believe God has made him a liar, because he has not believed in the testimony that God has borne concerning his Son. [11] And this is the testimony, that God gave us eternal life, and this life is in his Son. [12] Whoever has the Son has life; whoever does not have the Son of God does not have life.

That You May Know

13 I write these things to you who believe in the name of the Son of God, that you may know that you have eternal life. 14 And this is the confidence that we have toward him, that if we ask anything according to his will he hears us. 15 And if we know that he hears us in whatever we ask, we know that we have the requests that we have asked of him.

16 If anyone sees his brother committing a sin not leading to death, he shall ask, and God will give him life—to those who commit sins that do not lead to death. There is sin that leads to death; I do not say that one should pray for that. 17 All wrongdoing is sin, but there is sin that does not lead to death.

18 We know that everyone who has been born of God does not keep on sinning, but he who was born of God protects him, and the evil one does not touch him.

19 We know that we are from God, and the whole world lies in the power of the evil one.

20 And we know that the Son of God has come and has given us understanding, so that we may know him who is true; and we are in him who is true, in his Son Jesus Christ. He is the true God and eternal life. 21 Little children, keep yourselves from idols.

2 JOHN 1

Greeting

1 The elder to the elect lady and her children, whom I love in truth, and not only I, but also all who know the truth, 2 because of the truth that abides in us and will be with us forever:

3 Grace, mercy, and peace will be with us, from God the Father and from Jesus Christ the Father's Son, in truth and love.

Walking in Truth and Love

[4] I rejoiced greatly to find some of your children walking in the truth, just as we were commanded by the Father. [5] And now I ask you, dear lady—not as though I were writing you a new commandment, but the one we have had from the beginning—that we love one another. [6] And this is love, that we walk according to his commandments; this is the commandment, just as you have heard from the beginning, so that you should walk in it. [7] For many deceivers have gone out into the world, those who do not confess the coming of Jesus Christ in the flesh. Such a one is the deceiver and the antichrist. [8] Watch yourselves, so that you may not lose what we have worked for, but may win a full reward. [9] Everyone who goes on ahead and does not abide in the teaching of Christ, does not have God. Whoever abides in the teaching has both the Father and the Son. [10] If anyone comes to you and does not bring this teaching, do not receive him into your house or give him any greeting, [11] for whoever greets him takes part in his wicked works.

Final Greetings

[12] Though I have much to write to you, I would rather not use paper and ink. Instead I hope to come to you and talk face to face, so that our joy may be complete.

[13] The children of your elect sister greet you.

3 JOHN 1

Greeting

[1] The elder to the beloved Gaius, whom I love in truth.

[2] Beloved, I pray that all may go well with you and that you may be in good health, as it goes well with your soul. [3] For I rejoiced greatly when the brothers came and testified to your truth, as indeed you are walking in the truth. [4] I have no greater joy than to hear that my children are walking in the truth.

Support and Opposition

[5] Beloved, it is a faithful thing you do in all your efforts for these brothers, strangers as they are, [6] who testified to your love before the church. You will do well to send them on their journey in a manner worthy of God. [7] For they have gone out for the sake of the name, accepting nothing from the Gentiles. [8] Therefore we ought to support people like these, that we may be fellow workers for the truth.

[9] I have written something to the church, but Diotrephes, who likes to put himself first, does not acknowledge our authority. [10] So if I come, I will bring up what he is doing, talking wicked nonsense against us. And not content with that, he refuses to welcome the brothers, and also stops those who want to and puts them out of the church.

[11] Beloved, do not imitate evil but imitate good. Whoever does good is from God; whoever does evil has not seen God. [12] Demetrius has received a good testimony from everyone, and from the truth itself. We also add our testimony, and you know that our testimony is true.

Final Greetings

[13] I had much to write to you, but I would rather not write with pen and ink. [14] I hope to see you soon, and we will talk face to face. [15] Peace be to you. The friends greet you. Greet the friends, each by name.

APPENDIX: THE ATTRIBUTES OF GOD

Attentive: God hears and responds to the needs of His children.

Compassionate: God cares for His children and acts on their behalf.

Creator: God made everything. He is uncreated.

Deliverer: God rescues and saves His children.

Eternal: God is not limited by time; He exists outside of time.

Faithful: God always keeps His promises.

Generous: God gives what is best and beyond what is deserved.

Glorious: God displays His greatness and worth.

Good: God is what is best and gives what is best. He is incapable of doing harm.

Holy: God is perfect, pure, and without sin.

Immutable/Unchanging: God never changes. He is the same yesterday, today, and tomorrow.

Incomprehensible: God is beyond our understanding. We can comprehend Him in part but not in whole.

Infinite: God has no limits in His person or on His power.

Jealous: God will not share His glory with another. All glory rightfully belongs to Him.

Just: God is fair in all His actions and judgments. He cannot over-punish or under-punish.

Loving: God feels and displays infinite, unconditional affection toward His children. His love for them does not depend on their worth, response, or merit.

Merciful: God does not give His children the punishment they deserve.

Omnipotent/Almighty: God holds all power. Nothing is too hard for God. What He wills He can accomplish.

Omnipresent: God is fully present everywhere.

Omniscient: God knows everything, past, present, and future—all potential and real outcomes, all things micro and macro.

Patient/Long-suffering: God is untiring and bears with His children.

Provider: God meets the needs of His children.

Refuge: God is a place of safety and protection for His children.

Righteous: God is always good and right.

Self-existent: God depends on nothing and no one to give Him life or existence.

Self-sufficient: God is not vulnerable. He has no needs.

Sovereign: God does everything according to His plan and pleasure. He controls all things.

Transcendent: God is not like humans. He is infinitely higher in being and action.

Truthful: Whatever God speaks or does is truth and reality.

Wise: God knows what is best and acts accordingly. He cannot choose wrongly.

Worthy: God deserves all glory and honor and praise.

Wrathful: God hates all unrighteousness.

OTHER STUDIES BY JEN WILKIN

STUDIES ON OLD TESTAMENT BOOKS

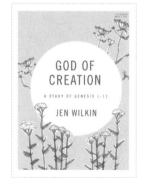

GOD OF CREATION
10 Sessions

Dive into the first 11 chapters of Genesis to revisit familiar stories and discover deeper meanings in the text.

lifeway.com/godofcreation

GOD OF COVENANT
10 Sessions

Walk alongside the fathers of our faith in Genesis 12–50—Abraham, Isaac, Jacob, and Joseph—to discern Jesus in the stories of His people.

lifeway.com/godofcovenant

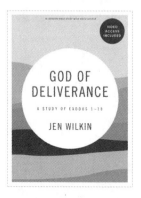

GOD OF DELIVERANCE
10 Sessions

Study Exodus 1–18 verse by verse to explore how God provided deliverance for His children to be able to worship Him freely and how it affects our lives today.

lifeway.com/deliverance

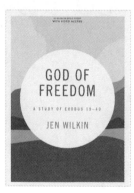

GOD OF FREEDOM
10 Sessions

Study Exodus 19–40 in depth to understand how the freedom God gives His children is meant to lead us to lives of glad service to God and our communities of faith.

lifeway.com/freedom

STUDIES ON NEW TESTAMENT BOOKS

BETTER
10 Sessions

Explore the book of Hebrews to learn how to place your hope and faith in Christ alone.

lifeway.com/better

1 PETER
9 Sessions

Study the book of 1 Peter to look beyond your current circumstances to a future inheritance through Christ.

lifeway.com/1peterstudy

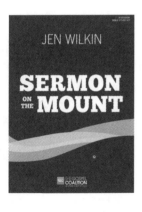

SERMON ON THE MOUNT
9 Sessions

Study Jesus's Sermon on the Mount verse by verse to learn what it means to be a citizen of the kingdom of heaven.

lifeway.com/sermononthemount

LET'S BE FRIENDS!

BLOG
We're here to help you grow in your faith, develop as a leader, and find encouragement as you go.

lifewaywomen.com

SOCIAL
Find inspiration in the in-between moments of life.

@lifewaywomen

NEWSLETTER
Be the first to hear about new studies, events, giveaways, and more by signing up.

lifeway.com/womensnews

APP
Download the Lifeway Women app for Bible study plans, online study groups, a prayer wall, and more!

 Google Play   App Store

Lifeway women

Get the most from your study.

IN THIS STUDY, YOU'LL:

- Study 1, 2, and 3 John verse by verse;
- Find encouragement in the truth that God loves you;
- Learn to discern the truth of God from a lie;
- Be challenged to remain steadfast in your faith.

Jen Wilkin's teaching sessions are essential for the learning impact of the study. This workbook is written to prepare you for the teachings, not to stand alone. Each 35–45-minute session unpacks fundamental truths taught in *Abide* and clarifies your study time questions.

STUDYING ON YOUR OWN?

Watch Jen Wilkin's teaching sessions, available via redemption code for individual video-streaming access, printed in this Bible study book.

LEADING A GROUP?

Each group member will need an *Abide* Bible Study Book, which includes video access. Because all participants will have access to the video content, you can choose to watch the videos outside of your group meeting if desired. Or, if you're watching together and someone misses a group meeting, she'll have the flexibility to catch up! A DVD set is also available to purchase separately if desired.

Browse study formats, a free session sample, video clips, church promotional materials, and more at

lifeway.com/abide

HERE'S YOUR VIDEO ACCESS.

To stream *Abide* Bible study video teaching sessions, follow these steps:

1. Go to my.lifeway.com/redeem and register or log in to your Lifeway account.

2. Enter this redemption code to gain access to your individual-use video license:

SSQG9WCQWWRX

Once you've entered your personal redemption code, you can stream the video teaching sessions any time from your Digital Media page on my.lifeway.com or watch them via the Lifeway On Demand app on any TV or mobile device via your Lifeway account.

There's no need to enter your code more than once! To watch your streaming videos, just log in to your Lifeway account at my.lifeway.com or watch using the Lifeway On Demand app.

QUESTIONS? WE HAVE ANSWERS!
Visit support.lifeway.com and search "Video Redemption Code" or call our Tech Support Team at 866.627.8553.